Cabbage von Dagel

By J C Williams

Copyright © 2016 J C Williams

All rights reserved. No part of this book may be reproduced in any manner without written permission except in the case of brief quotations included in critical articles and reviews. For information, please contact the author.

All characters appearing in this work are fictitious. Any resemblance to real persons, living or dead, is purely coincidental.

ISBN-10: 1535107278

ISBN-13: 978-1535107273

First Printing July 2016

Second printing October 2018

Cover artwork by the talented Ant Jones

Interior formatting & design by David Scott

Special thanks to Lucas Collier and Grace Maddocks for their creative input

Chapter 1

The 8th of February 1938 started unremarkably, well, unremarkable in that I was late for school, *again!* I could hear the school bells chiming in the distance, as I sprinted through the village square, doing all I could to avoid the hustle and bustle of the weekday market, skilfully negotiating the throng of people assembling, with the added obstacle of chickens and sheep.

"Late again, young Henry?" shouted Mr Noble, the market supervisor, with a broad smile. I barely had time to look back and waved a hand in acknowledgement. It was a cold winter morning, and my breath steamed into the crisp cold air; my thin school shirt and short trousers were little protection against the biting wind. My father's insistence that I take my winter coat now seemed sensible. The school bell had stopped ringing as I threw open the heavy metal gates and ran through the now deserted playground, up the staircase, and through the small corridor, slowing sufficiently as I passed the headmistress's office. I gingerly opened the door to the classroom, and fourteen faces stared back at me with a look of fear and anticipation, aware that one of their classmates was about to get shouted at.

Miss Grimshaw had already started to call the register as I bowed my head and approached her desk. I hadn't progressed more than two or three steps when she placed her quill onto her wooden desk and without looking up, raised her arm and pointed a strong finger toward the back of the room. "Get to the back of the class, Henry Maggin, and don't move until I tell you to."

I walked slowly toward the rear of the class wondering how she knew it was me. "What if it was the headmistress that had walked in and she had screamed at her to go and stand at the back of the class?" I wondered. I wished that one day that would happen, and the headmistress would make *her* go and stand at the back of the class. As I took up a familiar position — stood bolt upright — with my nose pointing one inch away from the cold concrete wall, Miss Grimshaw carried on with the register. Out of the corner of my eye, I could see my friend, Charity, cautiously waving hello. Before long, Miss Grimshaw told the class to remove their books and pencil from their desks. This was the only time we were permitted to open our desks before taking our lunch out.

I was startled by an unfamiliar voice, but as I was staring at the wall, I daren't avert my gaze for an instant. "Excuse me, Miss, you've forgotten me."

There was an audible intake of breath in the classroom. You never spoke unless spoken to... Never! I clenched my fists and winced in sympathy. The classroom was in silence for what seemed like an eternity. Eventually, Miss Grimshaw calmly spoke. "Tell me, boy, who have I forgotten?"

"Me, Miss. You've forgotten *me!*" came the response. He was confident in his response, very stupid, but confident. "On your feet when you address me, boy!" she replied, the calm voice now replaced by the familiar high-pitched shrill that would send a collective shiver down our spines. I could hear the chair of the poor wretch slowly being pushed back and could imagine his bottom lip beginning to quiver as he began to realise the enormity of his error. I tried to arch my neck to witness the unfolding drama, but it was useless. I didn't want to become the focus of the morning anger, continuing to stare at the wall.

"*Who* have I forgotten, boy, and why are you in my classroom?" she yelled.

"Please, Miss, I'm new. This is my first day," came the response, although now slightly mumbling.

"Your name, child, what is your name?"

"Von Dagel, Miss."

The classroom erupted in unison.

"Silence!" screamed Miss Grimshaw. My classmates soon composed themselves, and I could hear her moving toward the back of the classroom.

"Who or what is a von Dagel?"

"Cabbage von Dagel, Miss! It's my first day."

"Yes, you bumbling idiot, you've already said that!" I could hear the teacher, pacing around the classroom. "What sort of idiot would call their son Cabbage von Dagel?"

"My dad, Miss… or at least I think it was him."

I began to fear that this new kid would not make it through his first day alive.

"And what's your father's name? Radish?"

"No, Miss, my dad is called Horatio. Horatio von Dagel."

It went quiet again, and I was waiting for the thrash of the cane to come down, but it didn't. There was another brief silence.

"Sit down, boy."

I could hear the chair being positioned underneath the desk, and the sound of Miss Grimshaw returning to her seat.

The silence was soon broken by a familiar voice. "Please, Miss…"

"What now?" screamed Miss Grimshaw.

"Radish is my brother!" The class erupted again, and Cabbage was dragged out of the classroom by his ear.

I spent the rest of the morning with my back to the class, and as lunchtime approached, my legs started to buckle. It wasn't that I was deliberately late or slept in, but I'd been awake since daybreak, helping Dad tend to the animals, making sure they were fed and watered. When I was eventually told to return to my desk, I immediately looked toward the seat where the new voice had come from. It was empty.

My desk was in front of the empty chair, between my two closest friends, Charity Bernard and John Spaids. Miss Grimshaw had been our teacher for two long years. She was a tall woman — or at least she was to an eleven-year-old — with thin wire glasses resting on a large hooked nose. She wore her jet-black hair in a tight bun, so tight that it looked like it pulled her face back. Her long black dress and dark waistcoat added to her cold and angry persona.

The school day was long and tiring, especially if I'd been working before school and working as soon as I got home. We lived in a small cottage, which was part of the estate of Lord and Lady Evesham. My mum ran the house, and my dad looked after the gardens and the animals. We were lucky to have such a nice cottage to live in, because most of my friends, including John and Charity, were not as fortunate. John and Charity would often come to our cottage and were happy to help out with chores around the farm, and secretly we enjoyed doing it, but that didn't stop us trying to ask for pocket money for helping out. I never really spoke to the Lord and Lady, because like Miss Grimshaw, we were under strict orders not to speak unless we were spoken to.

Cabbage did not appear for the rest of the afternoon, but we discovered at lunchtime that he did indeed have a brother, and his name was indeed Radish. There were three classrooms in the school — Radish was in the first class; we were in the middle one, and there was a class for the older children. Everyone knew each other in the school, and there were nice children, but like any school, some not so nice children. Fortunately, our class had nice children in it. Our school was in the small village of Evesham, about a day's ride to London. Because we were so far into the countryside, new people rarely came. It was unusual to get a new child into the school, let alone two, especially ones with such spectacularly strange names. Although we didn't speak in the afternoon, you could feel excitement in the air, one that I hadn't experienced before.

As soon as the school bell rang, we raced out the front door. We were permitted to play in the school grounds until the teachers left for the day.

John and Charity were already in the playground and came running toward me. "What about Cabbage? What sort of idiot name is that?" scowled John.

Charity looked offended and pushed him on the arm. "I think he's funny."

"Is he your new boyfriend?" teased John. "You wouldn't have seen him, Henry, seeing as you spent most of the day kissing the wall again!" He was right, I had.

"Not tomorrow," I said confidently. "I'll be early, you'll see!"

I looked over John's shoulder, and in the far corner of the school, I could see Billy Steen walking toward one of the children in the younger class, who had his back to us. He took a look over his shoulder, and without any thought, he smashed this poor boy on the side of the face. I could now see the younger boy, Tom, was lying hopelessly on the cold floor, struggling to cry for help. For once, I was pleased to see Miss Grimshaw appear, and Billy casually walked away. Miss Grimshaw attended to Tom, who had blood seeping from a cut on the top of his eye, and looked around toward the rest of us.

"Who did this?" she shouted, addressing the crowd of children before her. I desperately wanted to say something — to point Billy out — but I didn't. Everyone in the playground had seen what happened, but nobody said anything. Miss Grimshaw told us to leave, so I waved goodbye to Charity and John.

I didn't enjoy how I felt on that walk home. It was cold, and the failing winter light did little to ease my guilt. I knew I could have said something, but I knew that Billy would have been waiting for me the next day. I took the usual route, through the market, past the church, and up the long winding lane to the cottage. I was freezing, but the sight of an orange glow through the distant window, and smoke billowing from the chimney, eased my shivers. As I got closer to the cottage, I could see Mum in her usual position, perched by the window, watching me walk up the lane, which brought a smile to my face. Mum and Dad worked long hours, but they always made sure someone was there to greet me and that the house was warm.

"Where is your coat, you daft so-and-so? You'll catch your death of a cold out there!" Mum brought me inside, and the warmth of the fire soon made me forget about Billy Steen.

"We had a new boy today, Mum. Well, two of them. Cabbage and Radish von Dagel!"

Mum just laughed.

"No, I'm being serious. Cabbage is in my class, or at least he was until he got told to leave by Miss Grimshaw."

"Cabbage," said Mum, chuckling to herself. "What does he look like?"

As I'd been looking at the wall all morning, I thought it best to avoid that question. Dad came in late, long after I'd gone to bed. But I couldn't sleep. I thought of Billy, and in my head, I wanted to run over and push him, but then I'd be no better than he was.

Morning soon came, and all too soon, Dad was ushering me from my warm bed to help him feed the animals. I don't know what time it was, but it was early, the sun still asleep, the sky as black as coal. We would always tread quietly to avoid waking Mum, but it was difficult to be quiet in a small cottage. We just had time to have a small bowl of porridge to warm us up before we crept out of the house.

"I believe you've started a vegetable patch in school, Henry?" whispered Dad. I looked blankly at him. "Cabbage and Radish, all you're missing now is beetroot!" he chuckled. I smiled, and despite the early hour, Dad was never tired or grumpy, as I was, most mornings.

I completed my work, and the sun began to rise over the distant hills, bringing a warm glow to the frost-covered ground. I kissed dad goodbye, changed into my school clothes and made sure I took my warm coat for the journey. I think I was on time, or at least, the distant school bells had not yet started to chime. I enjoyed walking to school; there was something magical about the countryside on a crisp morning. Fallen leaves had started to cover the ground, and the trees had a vibrant red glow to them. I quickened my step, eager to get to school early, and soon made my way through the busy market. "Morning, young Henry," said Mr Noble, his cheeks reddened by the cold morning air. I waved and negotiated the usual market obstacles.

The school building was an unremarkable, cold-looking building with a small playground. There was one main building, which housed the three classrooms and the headmistress's room. The classrooms were small and cramped and often had a damp smell to them. We were lucky, as many villages like ours didn't have a school, and children would have to walk for an hour or two — that is, if they were able to find a school to go to. There were a number of families on the edge of our town that didn't send their children to school. They needed them to help them tend the land or look after the animals. I was fortunate, and as much as I disliked Miss Grimshaw, I would always try my best at school. That is, when I was on time.

"Gotcha!" shouted Charity, as she jumped on me from behind. She was smaller than me, but agile, and used her size to sneak up on you with great effect. She would always have her blonde hair tied in pigtails, and was more comfortable playing with the boys than the girls.

"Guess what I saw last night!" she said excitedly. Charity lived on the other side of the village from me, but that didn't stop us spending most of our time outside school together.

"What?" I teased. "A flying pink rabbit? A cat with the head of a horse?"

"No, silly! After I'd finished my chores, I was walking back to my house. *Smash! Bang!* I heard the loudest noise I've ever heard. I looked for where the noise was coming from but couldn't see anything. A moment or two later, the sky lit up with all of the colours of the rainbow. It was so bright I could see the ground even though it was night time. I ran into the house to get Mum but by the time she came out it had finished."

"I think you've been drinking your dad's ale, Charity! Maybe it was thunder and lightning."

"Thunder and lightning? Since when have thunder and lightning been blue, green, and yellow!" she protested.

"There's Tom," I whispered. Charity turned around, and Tom walked towards us. He had a huge egg on the side of his face which was black and blue. He just looked at the ground as he made his way cautiously into the school. He was years younger than Billy Steen, who was nothing but a big bully. The guilt of the previous day came flooding back.

I pushed Charity towards the school steps. "Come on, thunder girl!" She continued to insist on what she'd seen as we walked into the classroom. Miss Grimshaw was already sat with her head pointed firmly toward her desk. We often wondered if she had a home or just lived in the school with the mice that would scuttle away as soon as they were disturbed. As usual, the classroom was bitterly cold, with a strong damp smell. It was dark as the windows were small and allowed minimal natural light in. I wondered if Cabbage would return, or if Miss Grimshaw had somehow made him disappear, such was her anger the previous day. The rest of the class had now arrived and taken their seats, and I assumed that Cabbage was no more. Just as the school bells started to chime, the door opened, and a small boy marched proudly in. He strode straight over to Miss Grimshaw's desk and confidently placed what looked like an apple in the middle. Without turning around, he walked past me with a smile and took his seat. The boy, who I assumed was Cabbage, was small, with the brightest red hair I'd ever seen, parted neatly at the side. He was wearing the same uniform as us — a white shirt with short trousers — but he had something around his neck. I didn't know what it was but later found out that it was a bow tie. I looked at Miss Grimshaw to see what she would do with the apple. Nobody had ever given her an apple!

    She raised her head, ignoring the apple and proceeded to read the register. I don't know why, but that apple fascinated me. I spent most of the morning staring at it, wondering if Miss Grimshaw would eat it.

    We were given 20 minutes to eat our lunch, and any time not eating we were able to spend on the playground. The sandwiches my mum had lovingly prepared were eaten in two or three bites. As I stood in the playground with Charity and John, I could see Cabbage by the school gate. I started to walk over to him to say hello when I heard a loud commotion. I looked around and saw Billy Steen pulling Tom by the shirt. Poor Tom still had the bruises from the day before. The rest of the playground had formed a circle to witness the beating that was unfolding before them. Billy let go of Tom for a moment and looked like he was getting his breath before continuing the attack. In an instant, Cabbage appeared. He stood directly in front of Billy, though was only about half his size. Tom took a step back, unsure what was happening, but the relief on his face was apparent

"You'd better move!" shouted Billy, who was also a little surprised to find this red-headed boy stood in his way. Cabbage ignored him, actually taking a step closer. He put one hand on his hip and the other straight out, wagging his index finger in Billy's face. It was hard to understand what was going on, but I knew it wouldn't end well.

"Naughty!" he said calmly, as Billy took a step back and looked around at the rest of the school, confused.

I'd never seen anything like this; it was the greatest thing ever, this small boy taking control of the school bully. I thought he must have some sort of magic power… until Billy smashed Cabbage right in the face. He didn't have magical powers after all, and, on reflection, was probably just a bit stupid. Brave, but stupid.

Billy walked away. I stood looking down at Cabbage, who was holding his nose — a trickle of blood seeping through his fingers. Poor Cabbage. It was looking unlikely that he would make it through a full school day today, either.

Chapter 2

The next morning, I thought of Cabbage as I took my usual walk to school, and for once I had the luxury of time. I felt sorry for him and secretly wished he had punched Billy, right on his big fat nose.

The village square was busy as usual, despite the early hour. I always enjoyed the frantic pace, with people setting up their market stalls, the warm amber glow coming from the blacksmiths and a smell of freshly baked bread. In spite of the hustle and bustle, it had a friendly atmosphere, but a small boy needed to keep his wits about him, or he would likely get knocked down by a passing horse or even worse, step in steaming cow dung.

I could see Mr Noble making his usual rounds, trying to keep order in the morning madness.

"Morning, young Henry!" boomed his voice from across the market. He always had rosy cheeks, regardless of the time of year, which always made him look jolly. I don't know how old he was, but he was bald with white hair growing erratically from the side.

He walked toward me looking stern, and for a moment, I thought I was in trouble.

"Here, young Henry, have you or your friends seen or heard any mischief out by the Stanley farm?"

As well as the market supervisor, he acted as the village constable, although I don't think this was an official position.

"No, Mr Noble, nothing. I'll be sure to tell you if they do, sir."

"Very good, Henry. Now you be on your way and tell your ma and pa that I sent my regards."

"Yes, sir," I replied with a puzzled expression. The Stanley place was the next field over from where Charity lived. Did he mean the lights that she'd seen earlier in the week?

As I ambled into the school playground, John and Charity were waiting for me. I took a look around, but I couldn't see Cabbage; perhaps he'd decided that the first day was enough for him. I explained the conversation I had with Mr Noble. "I told you so, didn't I?" protested Charity. "The sky lit up, and the cracking noise near on deafened me!"

Perhaps she wasn't crazy after all? Or less crazy than I'd always thought.

We trudged into the classroom as the school bell chimed. I was surprised to see Cabbage sat bolt upright at his desk. He was smiling, sporting his bow tie, and unfortunately, a huge bruise, courtesy of Billy Steel. I raised my arm and gave him half a wave. As I sat down and looked forward, I could see a freshly cut flower placed strategically on the corner of Miss Grimshaw's desk. I looked at the flower and then at Cabbage, who beamed a huge smile back at me. Billy Steen walked in a moment later with a sour expression, as was normal. Cabbage continued to smile, which grew as Billy took his seat.

Miss Grimshaw began to take the register but was interrupted by Billy trying to open his wooden desk. It was clear that the lid wouldn't open as he started to push and pull, harder and harder. Miss Grimshaw was getting increasingly annoyed by the interruption, as the whole class were now looking toward Billy whose face was turning redder the more he wrestled with his desk. Just as Miss Grimshaw took to her feet, the lid came loose, and Billy fell forward. At that exact moment, there was a bang — louder than I'd ever heard. A large cloud of smoke emerged from his desk, which for a moment made it impossible to see Billy or what had caused the noise. After a few moments, the smoke began to clear. Billy was sat at his desk, covered head to foot in a brown, sticky mess. He stood slowly, and the extent of the mess was clear. He raised his hands and carefully rubbed his eyes, leaving two small holes in the brown mask. Nobody was exactly sure what had happened. The smell took a few moments longer to reach the position I was sat in. As the smell reached me, Charity screamed. "Cow POOOOH!" as the entire class erupted into uncontrolled laughter. Billy stood for what seemed an age, as the contents of his desk spilt onto the floor.

"Get out of here, Billy Steen!" screamed Miss Grimshaw. He trudged slowly, leaving a pungent trail in his wake. As I continued to laugh, I looked toward Cabbage, who still wore the exact same happy expression. He didn't seem surprised by the exploding desk.

I've never seen Miss Grimshaw look angrier as she did that day, and being as miserable as she was, that is saying something. As she wasn't sure who was responsible, or in fact, what exactly had happened, we were all guilty and spent the rest of the morning cleaning manure. I was surprised how far it had spread, but we didn't mind, not one bit. To see the look on Billy Steen's face made it all worthwhile.

Despite our best efforts, we were unable to get Cabbage to take the credit for the exploding desk. We knew, or at least strongly suspected it was him. Unfortunately for him, Billy also suspected he was behind his public humiliation, but he was wary of Cabbage. Although he was quiet and softly spoken, and despite being short and wearing a silly bow tie, he had a presence and exuded an aura.

Cabbage left school that day looking ten feet tall, with a smile that had not diminished as the day progressed. As news of the day's events made it round the school, questions were rife: *Who is Cabbage? Where did he come from?*

A smaller boy joined him, who looked like an exact replica, only smaller, and I correctly assumed that was Radish. The von Dagel family had made their mark on Evesham school. It was certainly a first full day we'd not forget in a while.

Cabbage soon became a regular part of school life, and Billy kept his distance. He certainly wasn't afraid of him, he was twice the size, but was wary of him, like when a horse bolts at the sight of a field mouse. Our gang had always been Charity, John, and me, but as we got to know Cabbage, he became a welcome addition to the school and to us also. Mum liked him and adored his bow tie, suggesting that I might like to smarten up my appearance for school also. It was tricky at times because as he was so polite with my parents, they'd expect the same from me. The first time he met my mum, he shook her hand and somehow managed to produce a vibrant wildflower with the other one. He was quiet, not awkwardly so, rather thoughtfully so. If you spoke to him, he might not answer you immediately, but you could tell he was thinking. What he said would be useful, rather than small talk. He would never small talk, and to the uninitiated, you may think him being curt or rude, but this wasn't the case, he just wouldn't say something for the sake of saying something. I don't know if it was coincidence, but people seemed happier since his arrival. The atmosphere in the school seemed uplifted, and as the weeks went by, he even seemed to have an impact on Miss Grimshaw. She was still intolerable at times, but there were moments where the cold persona was replaced with humanity; no matter how fleeting, it made all of our lives a little easier. Cabbage still insisted on bringing her a gift each morning, and we would constantly ask him why. He'd been doing it for weeks without even a thank-you.

"It's nice to be nice," he would reply.

We didn't know much about him and his family, and he would never bring them up into the conversation. We only knew he had a brother because he was in the same school as us. As they'd appeared from nowhere, there were a number of theories circulating school, ranging from them being orphans living in an abandoned cave to being runaways from a travelling circus. I told people to stop being stupid, but in truth, I had no more of an idea than they did. I knew they didn't live in a cave, and just assumed the family were poor, and maybe he was a little ashamed of them. He would often walk part of the way home with Charity, and often insisted on making sure she got to her door safely, in spite of Charity also being a good deal bigger than he was. I asked her where he went afterwards, but she had no real idea either.

"He just walks me to the door and says goodbye. Mum always asks him to come in and warm up, but he never does. He walks toward Stanley Farm, but where he goes from there, I've no idea. I heard he lives in a cave."

I shook my head. "Enough with the cave. How would two kids live in a cave? How do they get food? How do they wash their clothes, and where does Cabbage find the gifts he keeps giving to Miss Grimshaw?" I didn't have a clue, and it wasn't looking likely that he would tell us.

"Let's follow him!" said John.

I looked at John, bemused. "Follow him? He's our friend. If he doesn't want to tell us why he is being so mysterious, that's his choice. As his friends, we must respect his decision."

"John's right," said Charity eagerly.

"No, we, well, but… Okay then, but this was not my idea." In truth, following him was probably my next thought, but I was glad that I'd not been the one to bring it up. It was drastic, but I was intrigued… and a little nosey.

The plan was set in place. We told our parents that we were going to Charity's after school. As soon as the school bell rang, the three of us bolted outside and took up a position outside of the school gate — out of sight. I felt guilty because I could see Cabbage looking for Charity to escort her safely home. He waited for what seemed like an eternity before ushering Radish and beginning his journey home. The depths of winter had long since passed, but the days were still short. The failing light worked to our advantage and provided additional cover as the three of us kept a safe distance behind the two brothers.

We soon reached Charity's house without being discovered. We crept with all the grace of an elephant wearing wooden boots, and I was sure the fits of giggles would alert them to our presence, but surprisingly, they were none the wiser. The Stanley farm soon came and went, and I was now in unknown territory. I hadn't been this far out of the village, and it was getting a little nervous as the remaining light slowly gave way to the night.

"This is where I saw the lights in the sky," whispered Charity.

This did nothing to calm my nerves, and it was now getting more and more difficult to see. "Think we should turn back?" I said in a slightly shaking voice.

"Scared?" chuckled John.

I was, but before I was forced to concede my fear, I saw a faint light in the distance.

"There, over there. A light, I think."

"Is it a house?" asked Charity.

It was too dark to tell, so against my better judgement, we carried on walking, well, barely a slow trundle by now. I could barely make out the silhouette of Cabbage and his brother in the distance as they walked towards the light.

"They've gone!" said John. "Where did they go?"

I quickened my pace, but they'd vanished from sight. As we got closer to the light, it was clear it wasn't a house, but what was it? Coming to my senses, I slowed, allowing Charity to take the lead. John was equally as brave, standing behind me, and at one point, pushing me in the small of my back.

Charity looked back at her fellow cowering explorers. "It's a door. Well, a hedge with a hole, with a door!"

She was right. The hedge was tall, twice as tall as me. There was an archway cut into the hedge and a heavy-looking wooden door. The light was coming from two candles, either side of the door, standing in large glass vases. Cabbage was nowhere to be seen.

I looked at John. "There're no houses around here?"

"There must be," he said with a confused expression. "Why else would there be a huge door leading to an empty field?"

"Cabbage must have gone somewhere!" protested Charity.

She walked towards the door and pushed it firmly, as John and I took a deep breath and a large step back. For the size of the door, it surprisingly opened with ease. We gazed at the open door tentatively, before looking at each other.

Charity shook her head and puffed out her cheeks. "You two are useless!" she whispered.

She slowly walked into the opening and grabbed mine and John's hands in hers, dragging us in. It took a few moments for our eyes to adjust, but we could see more light in the distance, and lots of it. As our eyes adjusted, I could see more candles in the same large glass jars. The lights appeared to run parallel to each other, forming an illuminated path, and at the end of the path, I could see the outline of Cabbage and his brother.

John strained his eyes and tilted his head forward. "What are they doing? It looks like they're climbing onto something."

In an instant, they were gone.

We hurried along the path to where they stood and looked down. It was a sheer drop surrounded by darkness, only broken by the occasional flickering candle. Above us was what looked like an enormous piece of rope coming from the distance, going through a huge metal wheel at the top of a large wooden pole, before disappearing into the distance again. We looked at each other, confused.

Before we had too long to think, I could hear a rumbling noise, which was getting closer. We all instantly retreated as the noise got closer and closer.

Charity squeezed my hand and said with a trembling voice, "What on earth is that noise?"

A silver object shimmered through the darkness, and in a flash, a strange-looking object stopped just in front of us. I ventured closer and could see it was a large hook attached to the rope, with a small platform at the bottom, with enough room to stand on.

"That must be where Cabbage went," said John, as he gingerly approached the object. "It looks like the giant swing we made down by the lake. C'mon," he said, as he had a moment of braveness and put one foot onto the small platform.

He held the swing in place as Charity and I cautiously joined him. I looked at Charity and gave her a smile of encouragement just as John lifted his standing foot.

Whoooooosh, we were instantly flying through the air into the unknown, as the structure spun and we gripped on for dear life. The sound of the wind deafened me as we hurtled downward, seemingly out of control. Through my watering eyes, I could see a similar object flash past us in the opposite direction, and by now, I was struggling to get my breath, and my legs felt like they were starting to buckle. The swing shook violently as it suddenly started to slow, and I had to grip harder to ensure I wasn't thrown clear. We came to a sudden stop, and I looked around, relieved to see that Charity and John had made it unscathed.

We stood for a moment, in shock, still unsure where we were, or what had just happened.

"THAT WAS AMAZING!" screeched Charity. "I want to go again!"

The swing squeaked as it moved gently in the breeze. Now I'd composed myself, I could see a similar swing at the top, so that when one came down the other must go up. There were more lights surrounding us, but it was still too dark to clearly see where we were. A path continued in front of us, but rather than soft grass, it was constructed of stone with a handrail either side made of rope. There was nowhere else to go. This must be where Cabbage had gone, so we reluctantly pushed on.

The adrenalin of the swing had left us, and fear had returned. The path stretched on for an age and seemed to constantly change direction with a strong slope.

John put his arms out, stopping us in our tracks. "There, over there. Look. Lights. That's a house, and it's huge."

"But whose is it?" asked Charity. "And how come we've never seen it before?"

"Come on," said John, moving forward with vigour. He was right; the house was huge, bigger than any house I'd seen in the village. There was a giant doorway with large windows either side, from which light bellowed out, gently lighting the ground in front of us. There were four large towers stretching towards the moon with smaller windows on each one.

"Cabbage lives here?" I thought, If I lived here, I'd tell everyone that would listen, and even those that wouldn't.

We ventured around the far side of the house where there were a number of smaller windows. We crouched down and slowly moved towards the first window.

"Ssshhh..." whispered Charity as she put a finger to her lips, "I can hear voices."

We cautiously raised our heads and peered over the window ledge, desperate to not make a sound. I couldn't see where the voices were coming from as the room was dark, only partially lit by the dying remnants of a log fire. I lunged back as a shadow crossed the window directly in front of me as Charity tried in vain to muffle a scream. The shadow stopped for a moment before vanishing from view. I looked at Charity — she was white. I was starting to think this was a very, very bad decision. My legs shook like jelly as I looked around, unsure what to do next. All I could think of was being at home, safe, with Mum and Dad.

I took a final look back into the house, but the shadow was nowhere to be seen.

"Come on," I said, as I gestured we move back to the swing and try to get back to the main path. I turned, but as I looked into the distance, I could see something silently walking towards us, panting, with breath billowing into the cold night air. We stood, frozen. A deep growl vibrated towards us as I saw a flash of white teeth.

"Ruuuuunnnnnn!" screamed Charity.

She didn't have to ask me twice as we turned and ran as fast as we could away from the snarling beast. A flash of light came from the house, and where it was dark, the ground was now flooded with bright light. A man stood about 10 metres in the direction we were running. He was dressed in a black suit, with a tall, shiny black hat.

"Freeze!" he screamed at the top of his voice. He pointed what looked like a giant gun with a huge, round barrel at the front, which was as big as his head. A huge, deafening spark came from the gun, and in an instant, a giant net had covered all three of us, the motion forcing us to fall to the floor. We struggled as best we could, but it was useless, we were stuck solid. I lay with my body pinned to the ground with my neck arched to see shiny black shoes moving slowly towards me.

The paces stopped just above where we lay. "What have we got here then?" came the slow, deep voice. I felt the net being pulled as we were dragged along the coarse gravel path.

"You lot are coming with me!"

Chapter 3

"What have we there, Wagstaffe? Bagged yourself a bunch of the Führer's spies, have we? Good job, old bean!"

"Yes, sir, thank you, sir! Found them skulking around the garden, not a moment too soon, either, sir. Admiral was about to have these three for his supper."

I strained my face, struggling to catch a glimpse through the blindfold that'd been placed firmly around my head, but it was useless. The voices were coming from the far side of the room. I had a moment of panic as I thought about what had happened to Charity and John. My heart raced as I heard footsteps moving closer to me. The blindfold was ripped from my head as I squinted my eyes, struggling to adjust to the bright room. I was instantly relieved when I saw my friends stood next to me. We were in the middle of a large room with no windows, and there were several large tables laid out in rows in front of us, surrounded by eight or nine people. A tall man in an immaculate green suit turned and walked towards us. He had a huge ginger moustache with vibrant ginger hair, parted neatly in the middle. He peered down at us, his left eye squinting as he stared at us through a monocle on his right eye. His face was kind, and I felt a wave of relief.

"Don't look like bad'uns to me, Wagstaffe!" He stooped down and looked directly at me. "What do we have here, then?"

I stood rooted to the spot.

"Quiet type, eh? I like it, you'll make a good spy with that stiff upper lip!"

"Please, sir, we got lost. If you let us go, we'll run straight home. We promise we won't even say we've been here, honest, sir!"

"Nonsense, my boy, you're guests. Wagstaffe, get my three explorers a warm cup of cocoa each."

"Very good, sir, right away, sir!"

I now felt more relaxed and looked around the room we were stood. Just behind our host, I couldn't help noticing a group of men working at one of the tables who hadn't stopped working since we'd been stood there. Standing proudly on the vast wooden workspace was row upon row of huge white swans. I could scarcely believe my eyes as one of the men started taking sticks of dynamite and putting them into the mouths of the swans — or at least I hoped it was the mouths.

Our host must have seen the look of shock on my face and let out a loud belly laugh. "Don't worry about them, my boy, they're not real. That's a swan bomb! Sail the little beauties right up the River Rhine — straight into the arms of Hitler — and *boooooom!* They won't expect a thing!"

I gave a nervous smile but didn't really understand what he was talking about. Wagstaffe returned and gave each of us a mug.

"Forgive my manners! Here I am, harping on, and I haven't even introduced myself." He leaned forward and extended a hand towards Charity in the first instance.

"Horatio von Dagel, dear girl. I'm very pleased to make your acquaintance!"

Charity nervously shook his hand. "Thank you, I'm Charity."

"Yes!" said Horatio confidently. "Charity Bernand, John Spaids, and Henry Maggin! In my line of work, it pays to know everyone in the village. You three are no exception!"

"You must be Cabbage's father?" I asked. I didn't need confirmation, as the red hair and quirky style of dress made it very clear

"Very astute, dear boy, spot on. You'll go far!"

"What is this place, sir? How come we've never seen it before?"

"It's always been here, Henry, you've just never been looking out for it!"

Our host took a step back and looked puzzled as he twisted the ends of his elaborate moustache. "You three have presented me with a dilly of a pickle," he said thoughtfully. "If you were adults, I'd have no option but to throw you in cells, as spies!"

"We're not spies, sir, honest!" protested Charity, with a nervous voice.

"Quite, dear girl, quite. Well, I can't lock you up, that's for sure. I must ask you to swear your silence, though. My young friends, you must not say a word about this place or what you've seen here today. If you do, I really will have to lock you up in the cells, and everyone you've told."

I shuffled uneasily. "Yes, sir, we promise. But in truth, we haven't seen anything — well, except for the swan bombs. What exactly are you doing here, sir?"

"Working for the king, dear boy! The last line of defence, keeping this fair island safe from all enemies — near and far!"

Horatio pointed to a large, ornate wooden sign hung directly over the doorframe. There was bold lettering, but from where we were stood, it was a little difficult to make out what it said.

"Ministry of alternative weapons and tactics!" he shouted with his chest puffed out. As he said that, everyone in the room stood tall and saluted.

"For the king!" they all bellowed at the top of their voices, before returning quietly to their work.

He turned his back on us and walked towards the door, taking a moment to salute the sign. "Come along, children, don't stand there rubbernecking."

We followed, deliberately keeping a safe distance from the explosive-filled swans.

"This place is huge," whispered John.

It was. The biggest building I'd ever been in was Evesham Hall, and this place must have been bigger than that. We were no sooner in one room before a door opened to another room, each one filled with people crouched over similar tables — barely looking up as we passed. It was clear that Horatio was in charge, or at least important due to the number of men that stopped and saluted as we walked by. "Very good!" he replied, returning the salute.

It was a maze of walkways, staircases and doors, and we struggled to keep up with the pace that Horatio was marching. The building looked like a palace, with huge paintings hung from the walls as giant chandeliers dropped majestically from the ceilings. Vibrant red carpet with gold edging added to the feeling of luxury.

He stopped suddenly — so suddenly that we nearly walked straight into the back of him. He stood in front of a huge bronze statue erected on a tall marble plinth. The statue was of a man from the waist up, smartly wearing a military uniform with his hat held under one arm as the other arm extended forward. Horatio put his hand towards the statue and with a firm grip, pushed his hand towards the ground. The wooden panelling behind the statue started to creak, and slowly a doorway began to reveal itself which opened into yet another room. We quickly followed Horatio into the room before the doorway closed behind us.

There were more men, working over the familiar tables, but these men were dressed in white overalls wearing large masks, which covered their heads completely. A tube connected a metal cylinder on their backs with the front of the masks. One of the men turned slowly towards us, and Charity stopped in her tracks.

"Don't be afraid, children," said Horatio as he placed a reassuring hand on Charity's shoulder.

"This is our chemical and gas division," he said firmly, as one of the masked men saluted in front of us. "This room is super sealed, so we don't blow up the entire village. But don't worry, you're perfectly safe. Well, if something does go wrong, you certainly won't have time to worry about it," he continued, smiling. "If this room goes up, they'll find our shoes on the moon!"

The man slowly removed his mask; sweat was dripping down his forehead, and his cheeks were the colour of a red rose. He went to speak, but paused, looking down at us.

"Don't worry about them, Corporal. My friends here are sworn to secrecy. Carry on!"

"Very good, sir," he said with a puzzled expression. "Progress is going to plan, sir. We should be ready with the prototypes by oh-six-hundred."

"On both projects?"

"Yes, sir, on both. We'd have been finished, but the men were, well, running a little low on gas."

"Beans, Corporal, plenty of the beans! Good work, Corporal, carry on!"

With that, the corporal put his mask back on and returned to the table. Our faces must have looked blank as Horatio continued with his journey. "Come, children, all will be explained." He moved us into the next room, which was cosy and more like a home, with a dining table and chairs, and a large open fireplace with photographs either side of a large mirror. I could see a picture of Cabbage and his brother and numerous other pictures of Horatio in various military poses.

Horatio gestured to the large sofa, positioned close to the fire, where a copper-coloured cat lay stretched and content, enjoying the warm glow from the fire.

"Ministry of alternative weapons and tactics, my young friends, is simply that. Alternative weapons and tactics — we think outside the box. We take the impossible and make it possible. My father had the proud distinction of setting up the department following the Great War. We like conventional weapons, such as guns and artillery. Trouble is, the enemy have the same weapons and know what to expect. The element of surprise has gone!"

Horatio paced the room with a stern expression. He paused in front of a large portrait near the door we'd walked in. A distinguished gentleman in uniform looked down on him, and I could immediately see the resemblance between them, and now also of the statue he'd shaken hands with.

"Montgomery von Dagel!" he announced proudly. "A great man! He thought outside the box. We've got the same weapons as the enemy, and the danger with that, children, is it becomes a numbers game. Who's got the most soldiers firing the same guns. Montgomery knew the advantage came from having something extra in the old kit bag, something the bosh weren't expecting. In the Great War, two sides would sit for days on end, firing the occasional shot, before some incompetent general would force good men over the top, to certain death, cut down by machine gun fire. My father took the best engineers he could find, and they dug. They dug for days in the freezing cold, under no man's land, waiting for tons of damp earth to fall on top of them. They dug a huge chamber right underneath the enemy and filled it with all the explosives they could find.

They didn't want to do it, but they had to, their friends were dying. They got to a safe distance and lit the fuse. They made more ground on that one day than they'd done in the whole war. He knew we had to think outside the box. And that is what we're doing here, today!"

We looked at each other with a collective, bemused expression. I raised my hand.

"Speak, boy, no need to raise your hand here, you're not in school."

"Excuse me, sir, what were they building next door, the men in the masks?"

"Bombs, dear boy, but not bombs like you know. A hand grenade does what?" he asked, staring directly at me.

I hesitated for a moment. "Em, explodes, sir?"

"Exactly! Explodes, every enemy for miles around hears the explosion and comes running, and before you know it, you're surrounded by a hundred guns. What we needed was something quiet, something that could clear a room without the enemy knowing what was going on, giving our men valuable time to sneak in and make a clean getaway. Those men are working on a flatulence bomb, a fart grenade if you will!"

I tried desperately to suppress it, but I couldn't and let out a loud snigger.

"Yes, very funny, I laughed too when I first heard about it. But like I said earlier, we make the impossible possible. We take the smell of thousands of guffs and concentrate it into a small handheld bomb. Silent but very, very potent, and it can clean a room out in about fifteen seconds."

"But, sir," I continued. "How do you collect—?"

I was quickly interrupted. "Something you're best not knowing, Henry. Suffice to say, we've got some men who never want to see another baked bean! We can be working on upwards of a hundred projects at any one time. My personal favourite is the sticky bomb. Gallons and gallons of jam strapped to rockets fly straight over the enemy and drop the payload, covering them in sweet, sticky jam."

"That doesn't sound very deadly, though, sir?" said John, puzzled.

"Quite. And exactly what I thought! The beauty of the sticky bomb is that we then unleash the hornets and the wasps — thousands of the blighters. They might not kill the enemy, but I can promise you, the sight of a black cloud of hornets will make you run. Most of them don't have time to pick their weapons up either. Sneezing powder also works particularly well. The men have developed the world's most concentrated powder, and one sniff, and you're sneezing for ten minutes, tears streaming down your face. Fill a load of balloons and drop onto the unsuspecting enemy, very effective!"

Horatio stopped talking as the door opened. I'd expected more masked men but was pleased to see a friendly face.

"Ah, Cabbage, my dear boy, do come in."

Cabbage was still wearing his immaculate school uniform, and I felt a wave of guilt. We wouldn't be here if we had not followed our friend home.

"I'm sorry, Cabbage. Sorry that we followed you home."

He looked at me and gave a gentle smile. "I'd have done the same thing, Henry. In fact, I'm surprised it took you so long. I thought once you'd heard about the lights in the sky that you'd have been here weeks ago. Also, you need to work on your stealth — it was like being followed home by a pack of water buffalo!"

"You heard us?" I asked, for some reason surprised.

"Heard you? It was impossible not to. But what could I do, I had to go home eventually, and if I stopped you, you would have carried on following me home."

"Did your dad make that pooh bomb?" asked Charity.

Cabbage looked instantly offended. "No, that was all my own work." He knew he'd said too much when his dad gave him that look that all parents were expert at.

Charity immediately came to his defence. "He did deserve it, though, sir. Billy is a big stinker — I wish we had your fart grenade to throw at him!"

"Anyway, we must get you home before they send a search party out." Horatio walked over to the door and pulled a chain that extended into the ceiling. A few moments later, Wagstaffe came through the door at pace.

"Take our young friends home, Wagstaffe."

"Very good, sir. Right away, sir."

Horatio walked towards us and crouched down on one knee. "I must reiterate — you must tell no one of this place!"

We vigorously shook our heads in agreement as we said goodbye and followed Wagstaffe through a further maze of rooms. He led us outside the main building, across the courtyard to a smaller building and pulled open a large metal concertina door. Inside were a number of cars, of different shapes and sizes. He gestured us to get into the immaculate car stood nearest to the entrance. I'd seen a car drive through the village, but I'd never been this close to one, much less been driven home in one. What a wonderful feeling as we drove through the small winding country lanes.

It was a long walk, but only a short drive back to the main village. "I'd best drop you here, save any difficult questions from your parents."

We didn't need asking again and jumped out of the grand car and watched as Wagstaffe disappeared into the distance. I didn't have a watch, but knew it was later than I would usually be out, so I made a dash for home still trying to digest the evening, which now felt surreal — like a dream.

It was strange at school the next day. We all knew what had happened but didn't speak about it. There was a feeling that we were part of something special, but something that we couldn't talk about. I looked at Cabbage with even more admiration, and I couldn't help wondering what other secrets he knew. I spared a thought for Billy Steen when I thought about how lucky he'd been. He really had picked on the wrong person, and I'm sure that if he'd wanted to, he could have made life a lot more difficult for the school bully.

When I returned home that night, Mum wasn't sat in the window waiting for me. As I opened the door, Mum and Dad were both sat, ashen-faced, looking at the fire. My heart started to race. I walked over to where they sat.

Dad stood and put his hands on my shoulders. I saw an expression I'd not seen before, it was a look of fear. I now started to really panic. "Dad, Dad— What is it? What's wrong?"

"Son, it's not good. It's just been on the radio. We're at war with Germany!"

I heard the words but couldn't comprehend them. I knew what war was, but I couldn't know about the true horror of war.

"The children are being evacuated, Henry. We have to send you away, to keep you safe."

Mum burst into tears and pulled me into her arms.

"I don't want to go, Dad. I want to stay here, with you and Mum."

"I know, son," said Mum, struggling to hold back the tears. "But you must go. It's the only way we can guarantee you'll be safe. You will have to go and stay with a family in the Isle of Man."

By now I had tears streaming down my face. "But when do I have to go?"

Mum and Dad looked at each other, and then hugged me. "Tomorrow, son," Mum whispered. "Your ferry to the Isle of Man leaves tomorrow."

I wouldn't forget the 3rd of September 1939 in a hurry.

Chapter 4

Rain smashed onto the cobbled streets as a crack of lightning briefly lit up the dark streets of Oranienburg, a small town North of Berlin. It was early evening, but the streets were already deserted. A street lamp flickered and swayed in the strong breeze as the sound of a ship's bell, moored on the nearby Havel River echoed across the town. A stray mongrel looking for an easy meal stopped and looked towards a small lane that led directly into the town square. The wind whistled through the abandoned streets but could not conceal the sound of slow, deliberate footsteps getting progressively louder. The dog, unsure whether the footsteps were friendly, scarpered into one of the many narrow side streets. The swaying street lamp cast an intermittent light towards the footsteps. A figure slowly emerged from the darkness — composed and deliberate — in spite of the atrocious weather. As the steps moved closer to the street light, the outline of a woman holding an umbrella came into view. She was immaculately dressed in a long leather jacket with tall, high heel shoes that echoed from the cobbled street. Her long black hair sat undisturbed by the wind as she continued her slow walk through the village square. Directly under the street lamp, she suddenly stopped and reached into her pocket as she fought to hold the umbrella upright. She pulled out a mirror and raised it to her face, giving the impression that she was checking her perfectly applied make-up, where in truth she was looking behind her to the route she'd just walked.

She smiled as she put the mirror back in her pocket and continued for a couple of further steps, before again coming to a sudden stop.

"How long are we going to play this game for?" she said without turning around.

She stood without moving and waited for what seemed like an eternity. Four men appeared from the darkness and crossed the square to where she stood. The men were dressed identically in dark leather jackets with dark brimmed hats — each wore a small button on their chest emblazoned with a bold swastika.

One of the men cautiously stepped forward. "Gratziella Machachella? You're coming with us, now!"

The woman turned and started laughing as she looked the four men up and down. "Four?" she said with contempt. "That's it? Four?"

One of the men slowly reached inside his coat as Gratziella moved towards them, her umbrella still held bolt upright. The remaining three men took a step back — a point that did not go unnoticed by the lead soldier, who was now starting to shuffle nervously. He removed his hand from his coat, which revealed the handle of a black pistol that flickered from the reflection of the streetlight. He repeated his demand. "You're coming with us, now! Dr Kramer insists!"

Her smile broadened. "Dr Kramer? You should have said!" With that, she pressed a small button at the base of the umbrella and with great precision, threw it towards the soldier stood in front of her. Startled, he instinctively reached for the umbrella, which was now directly above his head. Perfectly caught, it now protected him from the rainfall. Gratziella raised one eyebrow as he turned and smiled at his distanced colleagues with a look of pride. A scratching noise came from the umbrella. It became louder as he raised his head to investigate, and as he was about to lower the umbrella, it made a loud snapping noise. In a heartbeat, the entire canopy had wrapped round his head like a balaclava. A flash of white light briefly lit up the dark streets before a blast of smoke left the umbrella and drifted skyward. The man desperately struggled and tore at the canvas wrapped around his head, but it was useless, as he fell to his knees before falling face first onto the cold, wet cobbles.

The flash of light also startled the three soldiers, and for a moment they stood rooted to the spot. The soldier to the left regained his composure first and reached into his pocket to reveal a gun, which he desperately pointed in the direction of Gratziella, who stood composed as ever, as the rain poured down her face. The soldier in the middle made a grab for his arm and pushed it towards the ground, causing his weapon to discharge. "Kramer said to take her alive!"

The soldier on the ground managed to force the umbrella from his head and struggled to stand, as his head swayed from side to side — still unsure exactly what had happened to him — as bright lights shone directly into his face. Car tyres screeched as a car sped towards them before coming to an abrupt halt nearby. A man jumped from the driver's seat of the black car and also pointed a gun towards Gratziella. There were now four guns pointed at her, so she gracefully walked towards the car, close enough to the driver that he cautiously took a step back. In spite of the rain, she still stood patiently until the driver reluctantly opened the door for her. As he closed the door, he looked over at his three colleagues, shook his head with a look of disdain, and ushered them into the car. "Move! Dr Kramer is waiting for us!"

The car sped through the deserted city streets, and with the absence of other traffic was soon heading into the darkened countryside. The men in the car kept a cautious distance as Gratziella stared through the blackened windows with a vacant but determined expression. She was attractive in a stern, cold way, a fact that had not gone unnoticed by the driver, who arched his neck to catch her eye in the rear-view mirror.

The silence was broken as the driver reached for a stack of papers from a case underneath his seat. "We're here." The car headlights lit up a barrier stretched across the road, as two soldiers stepped out of a wooden hut and pointed their machine guns at the car.

"Halt!" screamed the lead guard. The driver pulled to a sharp stop and thrust the pile of papers towards the guard, who didn't avert his gaze. As he shone his torch and read through the documents, the other soldier peered through the window, looking intently at the occupants without uttering a word. The two guards returned to the barrier and slowly raised it as the driver nodded in acknowledgement and sped towards the lights in the distance.

The car pulled up in front of the house, and the car lights cast a brief shadow, which emphasised the Gothic-style architecture. Gratziella paused for a moment and glanced up at the menacing-looking gargoyles placed directly above the imposing arch that served as the main entrance. As she walked past a line of soldiers, an overzealous guard dog lurched towards her flashing its salivating teeth. She recoiled slightly but regained her elegant composure.

A soldier used the butt of his rifle to hurry Gratziella through the wooden main doors but was discreetly discouraged by his colleagues, who'd witnessed the events in the town square.

The soldiers strode in front of Gratziella and escorted her through a maze of winding, dimly lit corridors. At the top of a small flight of stairs stood a large imposing wooden door, covered in cast iron fixings, flanked by two further armed soldiers. As the party approached the door, guards gestured for the identity papers before cautiously stepping to one side. Gratziella was firmly ushered to the front where she threw a further look of contempt before pushing the heavy wooden door open.

The room was small and cold with bare stone walls, lit only by a handful of candles. At the back of the room beneath a large picture of the Führer sat a bald man in full uniform furiously writing in the journal in front of him.

"Gratziella? Is that what you're calling yourself these days? Please come. Sit, sit!"

Gratziella adjusted her jacket and sat steely-eyed. "Dr Kramer, always a pleasure!" she said with a hint of sarcasm, which did not go unnoticed.

Dr Kramer eventually looked up from his journal. "Thank you for coming at such short notice. I trust you had an uneventful journey," he said in a slow, whispered voice that sounded almost menacing.

Gratziella looked around the room and smiled as her eyes were drawn to a picture of Dr Kramer holding a large weapon, stood next to the Führer. Dr Kramer looked to where her eyes were fixed. "That was your finest work, Agent Six. An inspiration!" he exclaimed with increased enthusiasm. "The ultimate spud gun — firing entire potatoes at over two hundred miles an hour. A soldier could literally dig up ammunition. Genius!"

"Genius, indeed, Dr Kramer. I recall that you were quick to take credit for that one as well."

A stern look returned to his face as he slammed his journal shut. "Your country needs you once again, Agent Six. We trust you will not disappoint!"

Gratziella leaned forward slightly, her interest peaked. "Dr Kramer, it's always a pleasure to serve our Führer!"

"And financially rewarding," stressed Dr Kramer.

"Quite! I assume it is something to assist the war effort, Doctor?"

"You would assume correctly, Agent Six. The Führer wants to be stood in Trafalgar Square in six months, but we're concerned. Churchill is no fool, and we know he is planning something — we just don't know what."

"This is all fascinating, Dr Kramer, but where do I fit in?"

"Churchill has got his top man working on a special weapon, one we're told could directly shift the balance of the war in their favour. This cannot happen, Agent Six. We need you to destroy this weapon, steal the plans and kill the entire team, particularly their top man, someone you're very familiar with — your former mentor."

Gratziella pursed her lips in an attempt to subdue a smile. "Von Dagel?"

"Yes, von Dagel!" said Dr Kramer as he slammed his clenched fist onto his desk. He passed a thick file to Gratziella, which contained all of the intelligence the German authorities held on the secret weapon.

"You leave tonight, Agent Six. A car is waiting outside to take you to your transport."

Gratziella, as she picked up the file, nodding in acknowledgement. "Just one question, Dr Kramer, where is the weapon?"

"We don't know. We can only assume it is where von Dagel was last reported. Agent Six, you're heading to the Isle of Man. Failure is, of course, not an option."

Chapter 5

I didn't sleep much that night as I recall, thoughts of leaving my friends and family ran heavy through my head. In moments of clarity, I could understand why the children were being sent away, but Evesham wasn't exactly a key strategic target for the German invasion. I'd hoped that at least I would have Charity and John joining me, but the decision was taken that the children would be sent to different families throughout England; I later found out that they didn't want all of the village children in one location, which could potentially be bombed. This was logic, I would come to understand, but it was little comfort to an eleven-year-old who thought his world had just fallen apart.

I was woken early by Mum as a bus would take us to the train station which was about 20 miles out of the village. I'd only been on a train a couple of times previously, which also added to my anxieties. Mum was clearly upset but was doing her best to keep a positive attitude, and Dad was trying to explain how much of an adventure awaited me in the Isle of Man and that I'd be back home before I knew it.

The village square was bustling with people, but the atmosphere was vibrant as usual although cloaked by a feeling of loss. There were only a handful of children saying their final goodbyes and a larger number of men dressed smartly in their military uniforms as Mr Noble shouted instructions for us to board the bus. The occupants of the bus were being sent to various locations and like the men in uniform would eventually be sent overseas to hopefully put one right on Hitler's chin. As the bus pulled away, I desperately struggled to hold back the tears as my lower lip trembled uncontrollably. Mum waved before turning and putting her head onto Dad's shoulder, who blew me a kiss. There was a wave of optimism on the bus, which I'd not expected, particularly from the soldiers, which lifted my spirits. One of the soldiers I recognised as the older brother of one of the children in my school. He could see the look of apprehension on the faces of us younger children, particularly one boy who must have been no older than four or five. The soldier sat beside him and placed his arm on his shoulder,

"It's okay to be scared, you know. I get scared all the time. I'm scared right now."

The young boy looked at the floor and wiped a tear from his face. The soldier patted him on the back and gently placed his camouflaged helmet onto his head. It was twice the size of his head and covered most it, but it brought a faint smile.

I'd soon boarded the train north to the port of Liverpool. The train was magical and brought a welcome relief from the sadness of leaving home. It was packed mainly with uniformed soldiers, stood to allow the civilian passengers to sit. I was directed towards a carriage which had closed compartments with a corridor running parallel that allowed me to watch the soldiers moving throughout the train. There were two younger children and four adults sharing the compartment. One of the men escorting us smoked a large brown pipe that spewed choking fumes throughout the cabin, which clung to my thick overcoat that combined with the rocking sensation of the train, made me start to feel ill. I walked down the corridor where a window was slightly ajar allowing fresh air to come flooding in. I stood and looked at the green countryside which flashed by the window as the steam from the locomotive drifted throughout the carriage. I couldn't help wondering what lay ahead for me, and I felt lonely. The thought of being in class with Miss Grimshaw would have been a welcome distraction at that point until a shrill whistle echoed as we hurtled through a dark tunnel and brought me to my senses. I thought of Billy Steen covered in pooh, which brought a welcome smile to my face.

The Isle of Man was a small island located in the middle of the Irish Sea and popular with tourists and the world-famous TT races. Dad had never been, but he'd known people who had spoken about it fondly. When war was declared, the allies had the problem of what to do with the German nationals and potential enemies located in the British Isles. At the outbreak of the war, there were around 80,000 potential enemy aliens in Britain, who, it was feared could be spies or willing to assist Britain's enemies in the event of an invasion. All Germans and Austrians over the age of 16 were called before special tribunals and categorised according to their risk, and later in the war, Italian nationals also. It was often the case that those rounded up had lived in the UK for many years. Many enemy aliens were sent to camps set up on racecourses and incomplete housing estates in the UK, but the majority ended up in the Isle of Man in internment camps.

Four uniformed soldiers walked up the corridor behind me and stood about a metre away. I smiled, but all four had serious expressions, which I thought unusual. They didn't pay much attention to me and whispered to themselves as the nearest soldier gestured to a door behind me, which led to the first carriage in the train. I struggled to recognise the accent and assumed it was one from the north of the country. There was something about them, but I couldn't quite put my finger on it; the way they acted, stood, spoke just didn't feel right. The colour of the brown uniform didn't seem to match the other soldiers I'd seen on the train and at the station. The soldier closest to me looked at his watch and nodded his head as a second soldier passed him a phone receiver which was attached by a cable to his enormous backpack.

He fiddled for a moment with the dials, and then in a whispered but firm voice said, "Go, go, go!"

I nervously tried to walk past them, but one of the soldiers put his hand on my shoulder and pushed me against the side of the carriage so my face pressed up against the window. We continued to speed through the countryside, but parallel to the train, two dark coloured cars raced alongside, gradually pulling in front of the train.

"Hold tight!" shouted a soldier, and I instinctively grabbed onto a brass handrail, closely followed by the four soldiers. In an instant, the train lurched forward and threw me towards the front of the carriage — a soldier came with me and ended up in a crumpled heap next to me. A deafening, screeching noise erupted as the train slowed violently, and bags and coats flew through the air, narrowly avoiding me, but the soldier lying next to me was not so lucky as a suitcase hit him firmly in the face. I was still unsure what had happened, but the soldiers who were all now on their feet had armed themselves with pistols and stood in front of the carriage door. They spoke loudly amongst themselves, but now I couldn't understand them. I thought I'd banged my head so hard, but I soon recognised the accent — it was German.

The soldiers pulled at the handle of the door, but it was locked. Without thinking, the soldier carrying the radio reached for a brown tube — like toothpaste — but larger, and threw it to his colleague closest to the door. He squeezed the tube, and it made a popping noise, followed by a loud fizz. He quickly squeezed the contents around the edge of the door and took a step back.

He looked down at me and waved his hand to dismiss me. "Boy, you may wish to move!"

I didn't need to be asked twice and moved at speed towards the rear of the carriage where people were stood, looking confused and wondering what the commotion was all about. The paste around the door started to glow, and the fizzing noise became increasingly louder and started to glow like a red-hot coal. The door started to sway before crashing to the floor, fanning the smoke away from the entrance. The soldiers braced themselves and marched into the carriage where the blue light was coming from. As the smoke cleared, three men in white overalls became visible. They were crouched over a bench and slowly raised their hands in submission. The brilliant blue light was coming from four lamps placed in the bench, but other than that the carriage was empty. The tone of the soldiers became more aggressive as they grabbed one of the seated men and pulled him to his feet.

"Tell us, where is it? Where are the plans? Where is the prototype?"

The man in the overalls gave a wry smile. "Prototype?" he said with an implied ignorance. The soldiers looked at each other before one grabbed a blue light from the workbench and threw it against the wall in frustration.

The door directly behind me that connected the carriages was wedged shut, and by now, the unexpected delay had attracted the attention of the other soldiers on the train who were now looking through the window to see what had caused the disruption. The German soldiers were not stupid — the train was full of armed British soldiers — so they calmly made a final check of the carriage before sending a friendly smile to the waiting British soldiers. They indicated to the waiting soldiers that they were looking for something and made their way towards the only exit in the carriage. I tried to attract the attention of the British soldiers, but it was useless; I was lying on the floor, and they were looking over my head towards the carriage with the blue light.

The German soldiers left the train and casually walked towards the engine, where a large black car was parked straight across the tracks. The car had caused the train to come to a halt in the first place. Another German soldier jumped from the footplate of the engine and removed the pistol that he'd been pointing at the bemused and frightened driver; he joined them in the car and they drove off at speed in the direction they'd come from.

I stood and forced the metal rod from the door, allowing the British soldiers to access the carriage, and one of the men in white overalls walked towards them and explained what had happened. A soldier that had more stripes on his arm shouted instructions to the other men, and in an instant, several of them armed their rifles and jumped from the train, forming a perimeter guard around the front of the train, but it was useless, the Germans were now miles away.

The soldier with the stripes radioed through to his command centre to warn about the armed, enemy soldiers, and before long I could hear the distant sound of sirens resounding through the countryside. He walked towards the front carriage and examined the empty room, the broken lamp, and was surprised to see that the room was all but empty. Confused, he turned towards the man in the white overalls. "What exactly is going on here? Why would German soldiers risk their lives to sneak aboard a train — *filled with British soldiers* — to seize an empty room with only you three civilians and a broken lamp?"

The man in the white overalls nodded his head in agreement and placed an almost condescending hand on the soldier's back. "Son, good work, but this is so far above your pay grade it'd make your head spin!"

The soldier looked offended and stepped back, still unsure if the men in front of him were friendlies. Before he could speak, a letter was placed into his hand, which he read intently, before he puffed out his chest and gave a determined salute. "Very good, sir. I await your orders!"

I looked at the man in white overalls and recognised him — but how? I stared at him for an age but just could not place him. I was about to dismiss the notion when he looked at me.

"Stand easy, Henry Maggin, you did well. Solid stiff-upper-lip, good work!"

My confusion increased for a second before I had a moment of clarity. "Wagstaffe?" I said cautiously as I took a step towards him.

"Indeed, young Henry!"

I think Wagstaffe could understand my confusion as I'd only met him once, and most of that was being dragged in a net at Cabbage's house.

"But, what, why, what?" I don't understand, I mumbled incoherently.

Wagstaffe smiled. "In good time, Henry, in good time!"

With that, he dismissed the soldiers and gave them instructions to have the driver continue with the journey. Wagstaffe moved me into the front carriage and went to close the door before realising it was a melted mess, lying on the floor. He checked to make sure the area was clear before he took a seat so he was looking me in the eye. "Henry, I won't lie to you, you might be in danger!"

"How, why?" I mumbled — I was struggling to get my words out since Wagstaffe appeared.

"You know what we do, and this has placed you in danger. We knew the war was coming, but we didn't quite expect it to happen this soon. The Germans know we're working on something, just not exactly what it is."

"But I don't, either," I protested.

"Quite. But the Germans don't know that. The house you and your friends came to uninvited, well, it would appear the Germans have had that under surveillance for some time, so you and your friends are now potentially in danger, so you'll need to come with us now!"

"But, but, I'm going to the Isle of Man to stay with a family!"

"You're still going to the Isle of Man, but that family is the von Dagels. It's all arranged, and it's not a surprise you're on the same train as us."

"But what about John and Charity — my family?" I said with a wave of panic.

"Don't worry, we've taken care of it. They'll be well looked after!"

"But what about the empty carriage? I don't understand."

Wagstaffe smiled reassuringly. "We knew the Germans were watching us, but we needed to find out what they knew. We needed to know if they'd also intercepted our communications. You know what our unit does, and so do the Germans. We're working on something that will shift the power of the war, so the Germans will stop at nothing to get that information. The easiest way to find out if they'd intercepted us, was to send fake coded messages about transporting the device."

"So they must have broken your code?"

"Correct, Henry. It isn't a major problem as we've already moved on to a new communication system, but we needed to be sure — we needed to know they knew. Unfortunately, this may now place you in danger. At least we've exposed them today, and the local police will soon have them in custody."

"But what were they looking for? What is the prototype they needed?"

Wagstaffe looked through me and took a step back, saluting as he did so.

"Good work, Wagstaffe, I'll take it from here!"

I spun round to see the imposing sight of Horatio von Dagel hovering above me, dressed in a vibrant dark orange suit that almost matched his hair and resplendent moustache.

"Project H2Odour," he proudly announced in his booming voice. "H2O for short," he continued. "Guns won't win this war, Henry, and that's where we come in!"

He nodded proudly to himself. "Anyway, Henry, we're not going to win the war stood here! Wagstaffe, have the driver stoke the engines and let's get this Iron Horse onwards to Liverpool. We've got a ferry to catch to the Isle of Man!"

The train released a shrill whistle, and steam bellowed as it slowly burst back into life. As the train disappeared through the tree-lined valley, a radio crackled in the dashboard of a car parked on a narrow farm track on the top of a nearby hill. A hand covered in a black leather glove strummed the top of the steering wheel impatiently as a mumbled voice broke through the speakers. The gloved fingers came to an abrupt halt and started to grip the steering wheel.

"I repeat, Agent Six, mission aborted, mission aborted. The recovery team are being chased by local law enforcement, and we need an extraction immediately. We cannot evade them for much longer."

The response was not immediate. "Tell me, soldier, do you know what I look like?"

"Confirm, Agent Six? What you look like?"

"Yes!" she said impatiently.

"Negative, Agent Six, we were not briefed."

"Good, then you're on your own. Fools!"

She re-tuned the radio and a gruff voice spoke briefly.

"Success, Agent Six?"

"Negative! They must have known we were coming and moved the prototype separately. Have the team meet me in the Isle of Man."

Gratziella seethed as she started the car engine and began the drive through the twisting country roads. She headed north but knew getting to the Isle of Man would be difficult. They were sending everyone who was a threat to the country there, and here was potentially the greatest threat to the allies, proactively trying to get there; she couldn't just get on the ferry or turn up at the airport. She placed her foot firmly on the brake, and the car came to a halt. She paused for a moment and picked up the radio to the same gruff voice.

"I'll need to parachute in. Have a plane ready for me."

The voice on the other end just laughed.

"I don't care how you do it. Have a plane ready for me tonight at twenty-three hundred hours. If you cannot do this, Dr Kramer will know about it by midnight. Do I make myself clear?"

"Yes, Agent Six! Very clear!"

She pulled a bag from the passenger footwell, removing the contents onto her knee as she lifted a pile of passports. Flicking through them, she found the one marked "British

Citizen," and placed a thick stack of money in her inside pocket. She rolled her eyes and tilted her head back in defiance. Pulling out a pair of scissors, she looked at her immaculate long black hair in the rear-view mirror and glanced at a small bottle of hair dye. The current environment was far from ideal for a makeover, but Gratziella knew that she needed to change her appearance to avoid detection. She looked at her British passport and then at her now-short blonde hair in the mirror.

"Okay… Fiona Collier," she said, slowly double-checking the name on the passport. "You and me are going to win this war!"

"Von Dagel, your time is coming!" she whispered to herself as the car pulled gently away.

Chapter 6

Liverpool was bustling as the train pulled into the Exchange railway building. I'd seen the village square busy before, but this was something beyond comprehension. There were literally thousands of soldiers, civilians, and children moving through the train station like ants. I stayed close to Wagstaffe as I feared that if I lost sight, it would be impossible to locate them again. He led four uniformed soldiers, Horatio and me along the busy platform with the soldiers politely but firmly moving those who chose to dawdle along. In spite of the crowd of people, I couldn't help smiling as I caught a glimpse of a shock of red hair stood next to the ticket desk — flanked by two soldiers.

Horatio moved forward, took Cabbage in his arms and gave him a firm hug as he looked at the soldier to the left. "Did the package arrive safely, old bean?"

The soldier didn't speak but nodded in confirmation.

"Splendid, simply splendid!" said Horatio with a broad smile. "Wagstaffe, have the car brought round. We've a ferry to catch."

Cabbage was dressed exactly as he was in school except the dickie bow was more colourful, green with a shimmering silver running through it.

"Cabbage, you should have seen it! I nearly got shot by German soldiers!" I explained, slightly embellishing the truth.

"I'd heard, Henry. I understand the soldiers wouldn't have been able to intercept them if you hadn't unblocked the door. Father was very impressed."

Cabbage looked over his shoulder before placing a cold metal object in my hand, shaped like a fork, with a ball of dark rubber placed at the end. "Keep this safe, Henry. If you're in danger again, point the ball away from you and push down on this button here!"

It didn't look like anything I'd seen before, and I must have looked a little underwhelmed.

"Trust me, Henry! If you press that button, anyone stood within five metres of you will be covered in bubble gum. Not bubble gum as you or I know it, either — rather, industrial strength bubble gum that will instantly incapacitate them, and take about three weeks to get out. One of the team got this in his hair during testing — he's now bald!"

I cautiously placed the... *bubble fork*, in my inside pocket.

The *SS Mona's Isle* was a sight to behold, sat majestically in the River Mersey. Over 300 ft. long with two huge funnels, she could carry over 1,400 passengers with ease. She was old but had a distinguished career in the First World War, where she heroically transported troops in the Great War. She would sadly be called upon to continue her war career at the grand old age of 34 and would be one of the first ships to leave for Dunkirk, repatriating thousands of allied troops.

I struggled to comprehend the magnitude of the ship and stood on the outer deck looking at the fine vessel. Dozens of ships were jostling for position on the congested Mersey. The sight and smell was one that would never leave me. I stood in awe of the City skyline and could have happily spent the rest of the day absorbing the scene before me.

The steam engines — like the train — slowly roared into life and eased the majestic beast from her mooring, and progressed slowly up the Mersey and into the Irish Sea. The Mersey protected us from the elements, but as soon as we moved out of her channel, the ship faced the wrath of the Irish Sea. The wind whipped up the sea, and the boat seemed to struggle through the rolling waves, which were now covered in white foam as the ship rocked from side to side. The crew dressed in immaculate white uniform moved through the ship gracefully, barely breaking their stride. Seeing this, I stood up to replicate it, but was instantly thrown onto the feet of a passenger sat nearby. I panicked in case the *bubble fork* discharged, glueing me to this poor passenger for the remainder of the voyage.

Cabbage ushered me to a private area of the ship where his father and the rest of his team were located. They'd quickly set up the space as a temporary laboratory, and the familiar white coats were now on display. The men were crouched over a metal object about four feet tall. It was shaped like a household chimney rested on a transparent base, which had a multitude of wires and flashing lights running through it. In each corner of the square base were four smaller metal chimneys. After a few moments, four men struggled to lift the unit and placed it on top of a large metal object which looked a little like our bath at home, but shinier and more official-looking.

Horatio kept an inquisitive eye on the men and paced around periodically, peering over the shoulders of the men in white coats.

"Is this H2O?" I whispered to Cabbage.

Cabbage looked at me, surprised. "You know about H2O?"

Horatio looked to Cabbage, and nodded his approval.

Cabbage cautiously looked around the room and adjusted his dickie bow. "You know more than I thought, Henry. Yes, Project H2Odour. We've been working on this for three years!"

Once again I must have looked underwhelmed — I really must stop doing this — as Cabbage looked slightly offended.

"What you see here, Henry, is what the German army would divert every resource into securing!"

Horatio walked towards them and nodded his head in agreement. "Quite, Cabbage. Adolf would give his left leg for that work of art sat over there."

"But what is it?" I enquired; it was like nothing I'd seen before.

"This, dear boy, will bring a country to its knees without one solitary loss of life!" Horatio announced proudly, as he continued in his booming voice, "For thousands of years, armies have surrounded an enemy position and simply waited — cut off supplies, to the castle or the town — until the enemy have no supplies left. The enemy is usually too diseased or too weak to fight. A siege is not without loss of life, however. Awful affair! Takes years, sometimes. What we set out to achieve was a modern way of bringing an entire country to its knees without firing a bullet, which is expensive not only in loss of life but financially crippling for both sides. We wanted a quick solution where the enemy knew the outcome was a foregone conclusion so fighting was pointless. What we have here, my boy, is exactly that! — the perfect modern-day siege."

"H2Odour is as the name suggests," explained Cabbage. "One of the most important things in life is a fresh water supply. Water does not only provide us with drinking water but makes crops grow, animals survive, prevents disease and also provides everyday things we couldn't live without, such as bathing and washing clothes. This machine will effectively pollute the water table with a smell so repugnant it makes the water virtually undrinkable, and anything that is grown from it will also be tarnished with the taste — like rotten fish. Anybody that bathes in it will smell like a rotten trout!"

"Quite!" said Horatio. "But harmless! Nobody will be killed, it's just unpleasant — well, unbearable, actually! It will destroy morale in days and bring the opposition army to its knees without fail. A nation stinking of fish! This machine will irradiate an area of twenty square miles and enter the water table, streams, lakes, reservoirs. It's so effective that birds who are irradiated will then become a carrier, so it will then contaminate water suppliers for miles around. We calculate that twenty of these machines will contaminate Germany in two weeks, and we expect surrender the following week, especially as we are the only ones that can reverse the effects."

There were bits I didn't fully understand, but I knew I was part of something big, something important. "But why do you need to bring it to the Isle of Man?"

"A great question, Henry. Very insightful!" said Horatio. "And the answer is this — we only have one of these. This is the prototype and nearing completion. The problem we have is that we cannot get the reaction to work at the correct levels. At the moment we could just about make a bowl of water smell of fish, so we're not quite there yet! Imagine if your mum was making the best sponge cake she'd ever made. The ingredients are in the bowl, the batter is mixed and it looks and smells fantastic. The problem comes when she puts it in for twenty minutes but it just collapses and falls flat when it comes out of the oven. This is the problem we have. The ingredients are all there, but we just cannot get the final ingredient to work. Very frustrating! Ironically,

Germany holds the key to making H2O viable. Well, German scientists, that is."

"But they won't help?" I said.

Cabbage shook his head. "No, well not until now. There are maybe five people on earth who have the required skills to complete the project. Unfortunately, our efforts to complete it have failed. There are two German scientists who have the required skills. They were working in London, but acting as double agents, unhappy with the rise of Hitler. Germany thought they were spying for them, but in truth they were working for us, handing secrets to them, but only ones we wanted to be fed back to Germany — low-level intelligence. We were desperate to get the scientists to work on the project, but they were being watched, and we couldn't risk blowing their cover. The outbreak of the war has helped the project because we can now extract them and move them to the Isle of Man, where they can work without the German secret service knowing they're helping. These men have family in German, and if they were suspected of helping us, both they and their family would be quickly and fiercely dealt with! This is now the perfect cover!"

The ship continued to push through the Irish Sea, and I'd made a pact with myself to never step foot on a boat again. I was green and ill, and dry land could not come soon enough. I was delighted to see Douglas harbour appear, and the ship began to steady.

An impressively armed contingent awaited us on the harbourside with two full troop carriers and three armoured vehicles. The precious cargo was carefully moved to the armoured vehicles and the convoy quickly sped towards Castletown, about ten miles outside Douglas. The Isle of Man looked like the countryside in Evesham, and I felt strangely at home. I was pleased that I would be staying with Cabbage as the thought of staying with a family I didn't know was daunting. I kept thinking of Mum and Dad and hoped that they were safe.

I could see a castle in the distance rising high into the skyline; I nearly asked if this was Castletown, but thought better of it. It was *impressive,* with towers surrounded by a vast exterior stone wall. The convoy of vehicles pulled up, and a huge wooden door was slowly opened. Armed soldiers hurried from the vehicles to form a tunnel into the entrance of the castle. Huge concrete walls formed a narrow walkway to the main castle entrance, which still retained its original portcullis. As I walked through, I looked up to the murder hole, which in Middle Ages would be full of men dropping boiling hot oil onto the invading forces below. I couldn't help imagining what life must have been like in those times, travelling for huge distances and faced with virtually impenetrable walls with soldiers firing arrows and stones at you. If you were successful in breaking through the outer wall, you had boiling oil dropped on you! The castle had not been used in anger for a long time, and before the outbreak of war was used as the local courthouse and jail. It was cold inside and barely lit with huge thick walls that were as deep as I was tall. Vast corridors were lit by flickering candles and condensation dripped down the cold walls forming puddles on the floor. The low light played tricks on your mind, and again I felt fortunate that I was invited and not trying to storm the building in anger.

Gratziella struggled to open the car door against the strong breeze sweeping across the deserted airfield. She made a final sweep of the car to ensure that no personal effects remained and walked towards the plane, which sat about 30 metres away into the darkness. As she approached, the engine spluttered into life, which momentarily startled her as she'd had her doubts the plane would even be here. As she walked towards the plane, the sky lit up a bright orange as the car she'd just left burst into flames with an ear-shattering explosion. Gratziella didn't break her stride as a man wearing brown overalls and a flying hat picked himself up from the ground where he'd instinctively dived for cover.

She knew planes and looked with contempt at the ageing Avions Fairey Fox before her. She climbed into the single-engine biplane and gave a nod to the pilot to begin preparation for take-off. The pilot gestured towards the radio and pointed to her ear, handing her the headset.

"I wanted to check you'd arrived, Agent Six!" came the familiar gruff voice from earlier.

She knew he'd done well but was reluctant to show her satisfaction. "This is a piece of junk! Have the team meet me at the rendezvous point. I'll be there shortly!"

The engines roared to life as the plane bounced down the overgrown runway and gradually pulled into the air despite being buffeted by the strong crosswinds. It'd been a long, tiring drive, and Gratziella gratefully took a cup of coffee handed to her by the co-pilot. She looked out of the window, and the landscape below her was in pitch blackness apart from an orange glow from the burning car. In a rare moment of melancholy, she looked at the vast area of Liverpool below, in total darkness. Ordinarily, it would be lit up by a million lights, and here it lay in darkness, almost waiting for the inevitable pounding by the German air force. She rationalised it in her head by being a neutral; she didn't really care who won, so long as she got paid, and would go with whoever paid her the most.

The plane lurched from side to side, which made for an unpleasant trip across the Irish Sea. The Isle of Man was only about 90 miles from Liverpool, but the rough crossing made it feel significantly longer. Gratziella was pleased to receive the signal from the pilot to get prepared. She didn't need to be asked twice and placed a parachute on her back, ready to be leaving the plane. She was conscious that if the pilot had miscalculated because of the strong winds, it was likely she would end up in the middle of the sea, where, in this cold, she would not last very long. The pilot gave final thumbs-up, and the co-pilot opened the door for her. She made one final adjustment of the straps on her chest and jumped firmly into the night sky. The wind hammered against her face, and she struggled to breathe as her eyes streamed, making it exceptionally difficult to see. She panicked for a moment as she could see nothing, no lights and nothing to help her gain her bearings. The plane had not been that high, so she had no option but to tug on the cord. As she did, the parachute pulled violently, and it felt like she would be ripped in two. She still could not see any lights, but rationalised this by the absence of lights in Liverpool also. Through her streaming eyes, she caught sight of a small orange glow flickering in the distance, and with the absence of any other options, she made her best efforts to head towards it. As she descended further, it became obvious that it was the agreed rendezvous, and a large fire burned in the darkness to bring her to dry land. She braced herself as the fire moved closer, and she gracefully made contact with the ground.

Four men appeared from the darkness, all dressed in civilian clothes. Gratziella removed her parachute and handed it to one of the men to safely dispose of. She didn't want to leave it for someone to find and alert a search party.

"Welcome, Agent Six. I trust you had a pleasant journey!" said the man who took her parachute.

"Call me Fiona, and lose the humour. Where are we?"

"About six miles from Castletown."

"Castletown? What's that?" she replied abruptly.

"Where the people you're looking for are, in a castle in a town. Castletown."

"What did I say about the humour? When did they arrive?"

"Earlier today. What exactly are we doing here? We were told to report here and meet you and give you this."

Fiona looked inside the box and smiled faintly. "Excellent!"

"You don't need to know what we're here for. You just need to take me to this castle tomorrow where we're going to remove a child's new toy!"

Fiona could hear something in the darkness and cautiously moved closer. "What's that?" she demanded.

She looked down and could see a terrified-looking man with a piece of cloth pushed in his mouth and his hands tied behind his back.

"He's the man who sailed us across that horrendous sea."

"So why is he tied up?"

"Because we kidnapped him and stole his boat."

Fiona shook her head. "Make sure he doesn't get loose!"

"He won't! He's sailing us back to Ireland tomorrow so we can reach our extraction point. There is an old farmhouse over the hill, so we've got food, and we'll light a fire."

This was music to her ears as she was desperate to eat and sleep. It'd been a long day, and she'd soon have a meeting with an old adversary — one who would be far from pleased to see her.

Chapter 7

The castle was considerably less intimidating during the day. Cabbage and I stood at the top of the tallest tower and looked down onto the village square, which was bustling like the village square at home. Whilst it was a time of war, the local population still had to go about their business and mixed with the numerous army personnel who'd taken temporary residence in their town.

Cabbage smiled as he pulled out a long thin tube which had an eyepiece attached to the top. "This is the ultimate pea-shooter!" he proudly announced.

He placed a pea into the front of the tube and raised it gently towards his mouth — carefully looking as his target moved through the square below. He looked at the flag blowing in the wind and adjusted the eyepiece to factor in the movement of the wind. He licked the top of his lip and made his final preparations — pulling a small handle which looked like the trigger on a gun. We were higher than I'd been before, and the people in the square looked like small insects.

Cabbage didn't speak but pointed towards the far left of the square where I could just about make out a large sow drinking water from a trough. This thing was huge, and its bum was pointing directly towards where Cabbage was aiming. He blew as hard as he could, and the trigger on the peashooter snapped shut and fired the pea towards the square. No sooner had the pea been fired than the sow reared upward and let out a squeal that we could hear at the top of the castle. It was tied loosely to a wooden table, which was full of fruit and vegetables and this animal flew through the village square dragging the table behind it. A farmer ran behind the sow making a desperate attempt to dive on the rope — but it was useless, the sow was far too quick. The marketplace was turned into turmoil as people ran for cover and fresh produce was flung into the air where chickens desperately flapped their wings.

It was utter chaos as Cabbage and I retreated back into the castle down the steep stone steps.

Horatio marched towards us, and for a moment I thought he'd witnessed the events unfolding in the marketplace. "Ah! Cabbage, there you are! Come, come, I must introduce you to someone."

We walked into the main hall of the castle, and judging by its size it must have been where the medieval royalty would have hosted their lavish feasts. Armed soldiers were stationed at the entry and exit points and further guards were placed periodically around the room. In the middle stood the prototype I'd seen earlier and the familiar men in white coats. The room was brightly lit with a large number of electric lamps pointed towards the prototype. A large number of multi-coloured cables ran from it to what looked like boxes with a glass screen. These boxes seemed to have flashing words and letters on them, and the men in white suits seemed interested in what was written on them. Cabbage explained that they were called computers.

Wagstaffe walked towards us with a precise salute. "Morning, sir, the men are here, sir!"

There was something about Wagstaffe that really warmed to me. He was always immaculately presented and simply efficient. I'd obviously never met any royalty, but he spoke as I imagined they would.

"Very good, Wagstaffe, show our friends in!"

He excused the two soldiers who stood guard at the door and escorted two men through the main hall. The two men also wore long white coats and instantly looked towards the prototype in the middle of the room. I strained my eyes because I thought my eyes were playing tricks on me, but the two men were identical twins. Everything about them was the same, even down to the way they brushed their hair.

"Sir! May I introduce you to Professor Bobble and his brother… well, em, Professor Bobble."

Horatio walked towards them and extended his hand, but the two brothers walked straight past him towards the prototype. They spoke quickly and with great excitement as they crouched down and examined it. The brothers were tall and slim and wore huge round glasses with thick lenses that magnified their eyes. They both had silver hair, but their hairline started far back so it appeared like they had really large foreheads. One of them had a stethoscope hanging around his neck, and he carefully placed it against the machine and listened intently. The other brother looked at the computer screen like I would gaze into a fish tank.

Horatio puffed his cheeks. "Quite! Very good, then… Carry on!"

"They must be the German scientists?" I said to Cabbage, but he wasn't listening; he just stared in awe and carefully followed them to see exactly what they were doing and what measurements they were taking.

"Ahem!" said Horatio, trying to get their attention. "So can you get the reaction to required levels?"

They nodded their heads in unison but said nothing as they carried on reviewing.

Horatio appeared to be getting somewhat impatient. "Very good! How long?"

Wagstaffe could sense the frustration and whispered to the scientists, and then, "Two weeks, sir!" he announced.

"Tell them they have one week, Wagstaffe! Carry on!"

Security outside the castle had increased since the arrival of the prototype and the scientists, with armed guards patrolling at all times.

The German soldier tilted his head from the front seat of his car so he could fully appreciate the full height of the castle. He looked at his three colleagues in bewilderment. "You expect us to break into there and steal the prototype?"

"That's exactly what we're doing!" said Gratziella. "Now pass me the box."

She looked inside the box the men had brought to the rendezvous point and repeated the smile from the previous night.

The soldiers armed themselves with pistols as Gratziella opened the car door. "Put those guns away, you imbeciles!" The men looked confused and offended.

She gestured toward the castle. "The British army have dozens of armed men securing a castle that probably hasn't been taken by force in over a thousand years. There are probably dozens more armed soldiers inside the walls that are over forty feet tall and four feet thick. *What on earth* do you think you're going to do with four pistols and a single brain cell between the four of you? Honestly, what has Kramer sent me?"

"What are you going to do, then? Walk up and knock on the door?" said one of the braver soldiers.

"That's exactly what I'm going to do! Follow me!"

Gratziella walked towards the imposing castle entrance, which was flanked by armed soldiers. Her four companions hurried to catch her up, unsure what exactly was going on. She'd cut and dyed her hair, but was strikingly attractive — a fact that had not gone unnoticed by the British soldiers.

They smiled as she approached, but her expression remained stern, and she quickened her pace. The British soldiers gestured for her to stop, but she simply marched straight past them into the castle. The men now removed their rifles and blew whistles to call for reinforcements unsure of her intent.

"Freeze!" the men screamed in anger.

Her four accomplices were wrestled to the floor and now had three salivating dogs inches from their faces.

"I'm thinking this was not the best plan!" said one of them through the side of his mouth that did not have a British soldier's boot on it.

The soldier repeated his demand and fired a warning shot towards Gratziella that missed her by inches and ricocheted off the thick stone walls. This time, she stopped and stood with her back towards the soldiers, and in a stern voice she demanded, "Fetch me von Dagel!"

The soldiers looked at each other with confused expressions. "There is nobody here by that name. Now, on your knees!"

There were now six soldiers pointing their rifles directly at Gratziella, but she didn't waver. "Get von Dagel down here before things get ugly!"

The men laughed amongst themselves, and even her colleagues lying on the floor were starting to wish that she'd shut up.

It was deadly quiet as the steep walls seemed to repel all external noise, and the tension was palpable. Gratziella opened both of her hands and discreetly dropped six balls, each about the size of an egg. They rolled slowly down the gentle incline towards where the men stood, and were initially unnoticed. One of the soldiers eventually noticed them and took a cautious step back. They started to make a loud noise — like a rattle clacker at a football match — which became gradually louder before making a loud popping noise, which threw them skyward six feet, so they were head height to the men. Without time to react, the balls exploded and the men recoiled, but as they did, thousands of strands of clear fabric flew towards them, instantly covering them head to foot in what looked like a giant spider's web. Struggling to move, the soldier closest to Gratziella started to wobble from side to side like a drunken man walking home from the pub, before eventually falling backwards. The soldier behind was also unable to move out of the way, and they all smashed into each other before falling to the floor like dominoes. Gratziella didn't look around and now placed her hands in the air as she could hear dozens more footsteps running from the castle towards her.

Leading the troops was Wagstaffe, who looked and saw his men lying on the floor. The gate soldiers were unable to move as they were holding the four German soldiers.

Wagstaffe gestured for his men to lower their weapons for fear of a wayward bullet hitting his own men.

Gratziella looked directly at Wagstaffe and repeated her demand. "Get me von Dagel. Tell him Gratziella Machachella would *love* to see him again!"

"Why shouldn't I shoot you now, Agent Six?" demanded Wagstaffe.

She nodded her head in submission. "Yes, you could. And probably should. But perhaps you could show von Dagel *this!*"

Wagstaffe cautiously approached her, and she requested permission to take the box from her pocket. She slowly opened the box, and Wagstaffe looked inside. He stared for a moment and looked her directly in the eye. "Come with me," he said as he quickened his pace.

We stood in the main hall, aware of a commotion outside the castle but unsure what had caused it. The soldiers had all stood to attention and were braced with their rifles pointed towards the doors.

Wagstaffe marched purposefully towards Horatio, ashen-faced, and whispered in his ear. Horatio had a look of anger on his face, and his cheeks reddened.

Two soldiers escorted Gratziella into the main hall, and she smiled sarcastically towards Horatio. "My old friend," she said slowly. "What a pleasure to see you!"

Horatio could barely contain his anger. "I should have you shot right now, and you're a traitor and a disgrace!"

"Traitor? I'm not British, von Dagel. How could I possibly be considered a traitor? I did it purely for the money — the Germans paid more than you did!"

"But I treated you like family, I taught you all I knew. You betrayed me if not your country."

She paused for a moment as if the words had resonated. "It wasn't personal. It was purely business."

"What do you want?" demanded Horatio.

"You and the prototype, and I'll be on my way!"

Wagstaffe took the box from her and showed the contents to Horatio. He lifted the lid and stared into the small box. He stared for an age before slowly looking towards Gratziella with a look of pure anger.

Gratziella repeated her request. "I'll take the prototype, and you, now, if you would be so kind!"

Why didn't he shoot her? I kept thinking. What was in the box?

Horatio looked around the room and walked slowly towards her. "Give her the prototype," he demanded. Everybody in the room looked at each other in confusion.

"Do it!" he shouted. "Do it now!"

"I'll come with you," he said to Gratziella. "My men will give you the prototype."

"No!" shouted Cabbage, who tried to run towards him but was prevented by one of the soldiers. "Why are you doing this?" he screamed.

Horatio walked towards Cabbage with a hopeful expression. "Son, it's your mother, she's alive. That woman has her. I have to give her the prototype."

Cabbage could not digest the information he was being given and stared vacantly at his father.

Gratziella smiled intently. "Excellent! Von Dagel, let's go, we've got a long journey ahead of us."

One of the scientists in a white coat looked on in horror. "You're not just going to hand over years of work!" He took a rifle and pointed it directly towards Gratziella as he hurried towards her. "You're going nowhere!"

The scientist stared in anger at Gratziella, and for a moment it looked like he might pull the trigger. Wagstaffe slowly walked towards them and pulled the pistol from his waist, also pointing it towards Gratziella.

Wagstaffe closed his eyes briefly before slowly moving the pistol until it pointed at the scientist. He cocked the trigger. "I'm sorry, but I must insist you put your weapon down. You don't need to get hurt."

Wagstaffe avoided eye contact with Horatio, who had a look of complete disappointment rather than anger. "How could you, dear boy? How could you?"

"Sir, nothing personal, sir!"

Horatio shook his head. He looked like a broken man.

"Excellent," said Gratziella. "Excellent work. Now, we must go. We have a long journey ahead of us! Von Dagel, let's go!"

"You're taking the wrong von Dagel," said Wagstaffe. Gratziella looked confused, and Horatio had a look of instant anger.

"Wagstaffe, no! Please!" pleaded Horatio.

Wagstaffe looked towards Gratziella. "If you want the brains, you don't need Horatio, you need Cabbage. He's the real power behind this project!"

Gratziella motioned towards her men, who by now had escaped the boots of the British soldiers, and they grabbed Cabbage and the prototype.

"Don't do this! Take *me!*" said Horatio. "I'll tell you what I know."

"That's a generous offer, sir, but in truth, we know that's not exactly a lot!"

"We go!" shouted Gratziella as she marched out of the room followed by her men. Cabbage looked and smiled at his father as he was escorted towards the exit along with the prototype. Wagstaffe also looked at Horatio with an expression of guilt, but said nothing, as he joined his new allies.

Horatio sat and put his head in his hands. "You fool!" shouted the scientist who'd held the rifle. "You've just given years of work to the enemy!"

Horatio looked up and spoke slowly. "You and I both know that prototype is useless! We've been working on it for years. It will never be viable."

The scientist looked confused. "But, why have we brought it here, why have we been working on it? What about those two German scientists? Is this some game?"

"Almost, old bean, almost."

Horatio stood up, looked the scientist in the eye and placed a reassuring hand on his shoulder. "The prototype would never work. The Germans didn't know that, however, they thought that we were on the cusp of something huge — something that would bring the balance of power to the allies. We knew that they would stop at nothing to get this. They knew the only way to get this was to blackmail me, which is exactly what they did!"

"That's fine," said the scientist. "I'm pleased your wife is still alive, but you risked our lives for a prototype that you think will never work. You wasted our time!"

"No, dear boy, what we've done here is vital for the war effort. My wife, Violet von Dagel, is the single greatest scientific brain in a generation. Simply outstanding. To have her in the enemy's hands is unthinkable, as she is the true power behind the ministry for alternative weapons and tactics. Gratziella worked with us and worked well — she was ruthless but effective, and what a team we made. That is until Gratziella betrayed us. She betrayed the ministry and handed our greatest asset over to the enemy. She handed my wife and Cabbage's mother over to the enemy. We leaked information to the Germans to make them think we were close to arming the prototype. The only leverage we had to know she was still alive was the prototype."

"But you've just given it away!"

"Quite! But Gratziella will be taking it straight back to Germany. The only person in Germany with the ability to arm the device is Violet. If we follow the prototype, it will lead us directly to her. It was the only option we had. We don't have long, though. They'll soon figure out the prototype is unviable. Wagstaffe is unfortunate — I didn't see that coming — and he knows everything that I know. But we must proceed with the plan, we must get Cabbage and Violet back. We couldn't get the prototype to work, but the combined brainpower of Cabbage and Violet could very well achieve it. Or, if not H2Odour, then something equally as catastrophic!"

Horatio walked towards the computer screen and pressed a button. A red light began to flash on the screen. "The prototype has a beacon inside it, and we can track the prototype all the way back to Germany! What better person to bring us to Violet than her own sister!"

Chapter 8

Dr Kramer stood bolt upright as a team of assistants pulled and adjusted his immaculate new uniform with a vast array of polished medals pinned to his chest. He could hear the expectant crowd gathering outside his window as he looked proudly at the picture of him stood next to the Führer. Gratziella looked at him with disdain and knew that his success was as a result of her own. This was often the case with powerful men whose ambition was achieved by climbing on the backs of others.

"Propaganda, Agent Six! Never underestimate the power of propaganda. Those slack-jawed fools stood outside in the village square will believe what they're told. If we tell them we're winning the war, they'll believe it, and the power of positivity is infectious! All they need is a little good news story now and then, such as the sinking of a British ship or the capture of an important general. I cannot tell you how good that is for morale — it makes soldiers fight harder."

Gratziella rolled her eyes looking at Dr Kramer as he placed a black peak hat on his bald head. He took a handkerchief from his pocket and cleaned his thin, round wired glasses. "The Führer was delighted that *I'd* captured the prototype for him and the leading scientific minds that the allies have. I've told him that his aspirations to be stood in Trafalgar Square are now in sight!"

One of his assistants looked at his watch and gently ushered Dr Kramer towards the balcony. "Please. Dr Kramer. Your adoring public wants to see the man that captured the enemy weapon *single-handedly!*"

Gratziella smiled; it was nothing more than she'd expected, but in truth she didn't care as she was being paid handsomely.

Dr Kramer adjusted his jacket, puffed out his chest and strode confidently onto the balcony in view of the large crowd of civilians below. It was evident from their expressions that they didn't really know why they were there or particularly who the uniformed man on the balcony was. The numerous soldiers surrounding the crowd and also amongst them applauded and cheered wildly, cajoling any civilian near them to share the enthusiasm. Camera flashes lit up the square as photographers captured the celebration from every angle with images that would appear on the front pages of the German newspapers. Dr Kramer relished the attention, fabricated or not, and waved to his seemingly adoring crowds below. Three Messerschmitt Bf 109 fighter aircraft flew overhead to provide an aerial salute. It was all too much for Gratziella, who turned to walk out of the room. An assistant cautiously stood in her path in an almost apologetic attempt. "Dr Kramer would like you to stay as his guest, Fräulein!"

Gratziella looked at him contemptuously and knew that she could snap his neck like a dried twig, but their current location was not ideal. She graciously accepted the invitation.

Dr Kramer returned from the balcony with a smug expression. He snapped his fingers, and his assistant came to attention. "Bring in our guest," he said in his whispered voice.

Wagstaffe appeared in civilian dress, which made him look uncomfortable. He gently ushered Cabbage forward, who looked remarkably calm considering he'd been kidnapped, sailed across the Irish Sea in a fishing boat, and flown directly into the heart of Germany.

"Come, come, Cabbage, don't be afraid. You're very welcome here, you're among friends. You, my young friend, are going to help me activate the prototype."

Cabbage looked surprised and a little confused. "But I cannot help you. If I could, I'd have already done it."

Dr Kramer looked towards Wagstaffe, who nodded his head. "He's telling the truth, Dr Kramer; he's been working on this for weeks, and they couldn't get the required reaction."

"So what use is he to me?" screamed Dr Kramer. "I've told the Führer this prototype will be ready for use in two weeks! If this child cannot help me, why did you bring him here?"

Wagstaffe shuffled nervously. "Well, Herr Doctor, Cabbage cannot help, but there is one who can — Violet von Dagel."

Dr Kramer smiled and rubbed his hands together. "Excellent, excellent! Fetch me von Dagel," he demanded. "You may be of some use to me, Wagstaffe!"

Cabbage looked nervously towards the door. He'd not seen his mother for a long time and had thought she'd been killed by the Germans. His father had remained positive, but as further time elapsed, they both thought that it was hopeless. A soldier entered the room, and directly behind him stood Violet von Dagel. She was short with blonde bobbed hair, wearing an unremarkable grey dress. She looked across the room and struggled to believe what she was seeing. Her solemn face instantly lit up as she shook off the soldier who was holding her arm and sprinted across the room. "Cabbage!" she shouted as tears ran down her cheek.

She knelt down and took her beloved son in her arms. "I never thought I'd see you again, son. But I never gave up hope!"

"How nice," said Dr Kramer sarcastically. "Bring her to me."

Violet gave a reassuring smile to Cabbage as Dr Kramer pulled a large white cloth away, revealing the prototype.

He pointed towards the table and gently whispered, "You're going to arm this prototype, Mrs von Dagel."

At that moment, Violet caught sight of Gratziella stood on the other side of the room. Without saying a word, she hurried towards her and slapped her in the face as hard as she could.

Gratziella barely flinched in spite of the strength of the strike. "I'll let you have that one, Violet. I deserved it. But don't try for another one."

"You betrayed me! How could you do that? You gave your own sister up to the Germans, and now it looks like you've also given your nephew to them. What sort of a monster are you?"

For once, Gratziella looked subdued and said nothing, looking at the floor.

"Enough distraction!" shouted Dr Kramer. "We've got important business to attend to. Von Dagel, can you get this prototype armed?"

Violet looked at the device before her, which had changed almost beyond recognition from when she initially developed the concept. She looked closely and shook her head. "No, it's not possible."

Dr Kramer smiled. "I thought you might say that!" In an instant, he grabbed Cabbage and pointed a pistol directly at him. "Perhaps this might focus your attention."

Violet stood firm as Dr Kramer pulled the trigger back on his gun. "No, wait!" she screamed. "Wait! I'll do it, but don't hurt my son."

"Excellent!" said Dr Kramer. "A little motivation always works."

Gratziella wiped a trickle of blood from her lip and strode towards Dr Kramer. "You really are an idiot, aren't you! That prototype is about as useless as you are!" She leaned backwards and with all her might punched Kramer on the tip of his chin, sending him crashing to the floor. The soldier was panic-stricken as he desperately fumbled for his rifle. "Halt!" he screamed as he raised the rifle towards Gratziella. He activated the bolt action on his weapon and the bullet could be entering the chamber of the gun. His finger lurched towards the trigger, and Gratziella stood still, almost accepting her fate.

She closed her eyes and heard a loud smashing noise. Conscious she was still upright, she slowly opened her right eye and could see the soldier lying on the floor next to Dr Kramer. Wagstaffe held the handle of a large broken vase, with the remainder scattered next to the soldier's head.

Wagstaffe quickly tied up the two unarmed assistants. He took the socks off the soldiers and pushed them into their mouths to stop them calling for help.

"You surprise me, Wagstaffe!" said Gratziella with confusion.

Wagstaffe regarded the men on the floor. "Do you honestly think I'd work with these clowns?" He strode towards the prototype and emptied the contents of a small bottle on it. The clear liquid sizzled as it made contact, and before long the prototype began to melt into a molten liquid.

"It *wasn't* useless," said Wagstaffe. "But, at least, it is *now!*"

The building was filled with dozens of armed German soldiers as Gratziella walked casually with Violet and

Cabbage directly in front of her. The soldiers recognised her and allowed her safe access through the building. Wagstaffe followed closely behind and felt like he was walking into the lion's den. He tried to exude confidence as he walked through the building and was relieved to see the main door at the end of the corridor they were walking down. Two soldiers guarding the main door turned towards them and looked them over carefully. As the party moved through the door, one of the soldiers put his hand across to block their path. "Halt!"

Gratziella didn't speak and was conscious of a bead of sweat sliding down her forehead.

The soldier paused for what seemed like an eternity before thrusting a picture into her hand. She was relieved to see a picture of Dr Kramer in her hand, waving like an idiot from the balcony. The soldier looked almost apologetic for handing the pictures out. "Orders!" he said with an awkward smile.

Gratziella didn't speak but gave the soldiers a smile as they left the building and walked through the village square, which was now empty.

They walked slowly through the square until a deafening alarm began to sound. Wagstaffe looked around and could see smoke billowing from the balcony where he'd destroyed the prototype. Soldiers pointed towards them and began screaming and blowing whistles, demanding their men apprehend them. Wagstaffe quickened his pace before they all started sprinting out of the village square. They ran until they could no longer hear the alarm; Wagstaffe was relieved to see that there were no soldiers following them. He pulled out a square metal tin — about the size of a matchbox and with a green screen in the middle. He pushed a switch on the side, and the screen lit up and made a beeping noise. After a few seconds, an object appeared on the screen, and Wagstaffe held the tin at arm's length.

"This way!"

The group followed Wagstaffe, who walked through backstreets as the beeping noise became louder and the beeps became less spaced out. Eventually, the noise became constant, and Wagstaffe stopped and looked around.

"They should be here!" he said with dismay.

They were stood on the bank of a wide river on the outskirts of town; the water stretched on into the distance as far as the eye could see.

Wagstaffe became impatient and walked towards the field behind them, which was covered by huge trees. The beeping slowed again, so he turned back towards the river where the noise quickened.

"I don't understand. They should be here!"

"Halt! Do not move!" came a screaming voice from the trees. Several German soldiers appeared from the darkness of the trees and directed their guns at them. Two of them had dogs, which were pulling at their leads, desperate to attack.

Gratziella attempted to walk forward to explain that she was moving the group on the order of Dr Kramer.

Her look of confidence was soon replaced with a look of resignation as Dr Kramer appeared from the trees accompanied by more soldiers.

"Agent Six. I'm disappointed in you. I know you didn't do it for the love of the country but for the love of money. I would have made you even richer! No matter. Shoot them all!" he commanded.

Violet stood in front of Cabbage as Wagstaffe placed his arm on her shoulder. Gratziella knew it was useless and shook her head. After all the many missions she'd completed, the disappointment of where her last mission would end was evident on her face.

The German soldiers raised their weapons and waited for the order to shoot. It was deadly quiet as Violet looked down towards Cabbage and smiled.

The silence was shattered by a sudden explosion. It was unclear where the noise came from, and the soldiers looked around but there was nothing in sight. A noise whistled from above, which became louder and louder until something hit the ground directly in front of where the soldiers stood. They took a step back, and the object in front of them exploded. As the smoke cleared, all of the Germans were covered in a sticky red mess, and they looked at each other in confusion.

Dr Kramer wiped the mess from his eyes and slowly licked his finger. "Jam? You fools think you can beat the might of the German army with jam?"

The sky suddenly went dark as a large cloud descended upon the German soldiers. Wagstaffe was as confused as the German soldiers and looked towards the sky as the cloud got closer and closer. The cloud made a noise, and Wagstaffe feared that the area was being bombed.

The cloud flew past where Wagstaffe stood and made directly for the German soldiers.

"Wasps!" screamed the German soldiers as they immediately dropped their weapons and ran in every direction they could to escape the wasps. In their desperation, they were running into each other and then into the trees. They eventually ran towards the river and with little other alternative they jumped into the water to escape the huge swarm.

Gratziella hadn't moved and stood looking at the German soldiers, covered in jam, voluntarily throwing themselves into the river.

At that moment, the water began to ripple, and Wagstaffe looked over the river bank. Bubbles came to the surface as the ripples became bigger and bigger. He took a step back as a violent noise followed the bubbles. The water seemed to part in the middle as a huge metal cylinder rose majestically from the water.

The submarine rose about three metres above the waterline, and the group stood and stared as the hatch at the top of the tunnel was thrown open. To their immense relief, Horatio proudly appeared before them.

"Don't dawdle, climb aboard!" he shouted.

The group didn't need to be asked twice and hurried aboard.

Horatio waited at the foot of the ladder inside the tower. Cabbage and Violet were the first to descend, and he took them both in his arms in a warm embrace. "I knew you were alive, Violet! I never gave up believing!"

Wagstaffe cautiously climbed down the ladder. To all of his colleagues, he was a traitor and could and should be shot on sight.

Horatio strode towards him and stared for a moment. "If you leave the forces, Wagstaffe, you'll make a very good actor! You almost had me convinced!" He warmly embraced Wagstaffe. "Thank you for returning my family to me, old friend. Thank you!"

"Henry!" shouted Cabbage, delighted to see his friend. "What are you doing here?"

"I wasn't going to miss this, Cabbage, not for the world. Besides, your father thought it was safer for me to come with him!"

Horatio stared at Gratziella with a look of anger. "Sir, if I may," said Wagstaffe. "We wouldn't be here without her. Without her, we couldn't have got out of the building!"

"You have my gratitude, Gratziella," said Horatio. "But not my trust! You will have to work hard to win that back."

Horatio popped the cork on a bottle of champagne and eagerly filled the numerous glasses, including a small drop, which fell into the glasses of Cabbage and Henry.

They all raised their glasses, as Horatio proudly exclaimed, "For the king!"

Chapter 9

The car sped through the streets of London as the sirens from the police escorts blasted in front of us. My parents looked proudly at me, and I blushed with all of the attention. As we approached Buckingham Palace, the soldiers raised the security barrier and waved the convoy through to the main building. We were quickly ushered into the Palace and all congregated in a huge room which was extravagantly decorated.

I was nervous but excited, scarcely believing where I was stood.

An immaculately dressed soldier pulled a trumpet from his side and called the room to attention. I stood next to Cabbage, and we exchanged a mutual smile. Behind me stood Horatio dressed in a splendid purple suit, which matched the dickie bow that Cabbage proudly wore. He held on firmly to Violet and placed a gentle kiss on her cheek. Wagstaffe stood at the rear and looked as efficient as he ever did.

The doors were slowly opened, and I could see an even more opulent room with a velvet red carpet that stretched out before us. Either side of the carpet were rows and rows of people sat on shining gold chairs all staring at us.

A further blast on the trumpet, and everyone in the room stood in unison as the king walked slowly to a majestic golden chair with a red velvet seat.

We began the slow walk up the red carpet, and I couldn't help noticing my mum looking at me with tears pouring down her face. I was even more surprised to see Miss Grimshaw and the other teachers sat in the audience. Miss Grimshaw had a warm smile which momentarily distracted me.

We all stood in front of the king, who gave each of us an award for valour in the face of extreme danger. He was unable to give any further details because, after all, the ministry was an unknown division and their work often went unrecognised.

I felt ten feet tall as I walked back down that red carpet with my friend Cabbage, proudly wearing the medal that the king had pressed into my chest.

Horatio walked towards me and patted me on the back. He looked at my parents. "You've got a good 'un there! You should be very proud." And, then, back to me: "There is always a job for you, Henry, we'd be delighted to have you on board. Be a pleasure to serve with you again!"

As Horatio looked at his friends and family, I swear I could almost see a tear in those steely eyes.

I felt something digging in my side, and, at first, I assumed it was my medal. I looked on the inside of my jacket and must have looked sad. "Why the sad face, Henry?" asked Cabbage.

I pulled out the bubble fork that Cabbage had given me and looked at it with disappointment. "I really wanted to use that!" I said.

Cabbage laughed and put his arm around my shoulder,

"There is always next time, my friend — always next time!"

The End

Other Books by J C Williams...

The Flip of a Coin

Hamish McScabbard

The Lonely Heart Attack Club

The Lonely Heart Attack Club: Wrinkly Olympics

Frank 'n' Stan's Bucket List #1: TT Races

The Seaside Detective Agency

Frank 'n' Stan's Bucket List #2: TT Races

J C Williams
Author

authorjcwilliams@gmail.com
@jcwilliamsbooks
@jcwilliamsauthor

Printed in Great Britain
by Amazon